SYLLABUS

Prayer Manual

By
Barron (Ronnie) Burch

New Life Bible College

Unless otherwise indicated, all Scripture quotations are taken from the King James Version of the Bible.

Excerpts from OUR COVENANT WITH GOD by Kenneth Copeland, Believer's Voice of Victory April 1980, Vol. 8 used by permission of Kenneth Copeland Ministries.

First Printing 1990
Second Printing 1994
Third Printing 2000
Fourth Printing 2012

New Life Bible College Prayer Manual
ISBN: 978-0-942507-28-7
ISBN (E-BOOK) 978-0-942507-51-5

All personal correspondence should be sent to:

Barron (Ronnie) Burch
P.O. Box 5528
Cleveland, TN 37320

Published by **Deeper Revelation Books**
Revealing "the deep things of God" (1 Cor. 2:10)
P.O. Box 4260, Cleveland, TN 37320
Phone: 423-478-2843
Website: www.deeperrevelationbooks.org
Email: info@deeperrevelationbooks.org

Printed in the United States of America

Deeper Revelation Books assists Christian authors in publishing and distributing their books. Final responsibility for design, content, permissions, editorial accuracy, and doctrinal views, either expressed or implied, belongs to the author.

DEDICATION

I dedicate this Prayer Manual to my Heavenly Father, His Son, Jesus, and His Holy Spirit—the three in one. To Mac and Louise, thank you for your faith in what God could do through me! To my children, Becky and Maxie, and their families.

And all things, whatsoever ye shall ask in prayer; believing, ye shall receive. (Matthew 21:22)

PREFACE

Prayer is the answer to all the turmoil in the world today. That is why the devil tries to blind people to the power of prayer. He wants to keep you busy with "activities" so that you will deceive yourself into believing you have no time to pray. The devil is not afraid of people who busy themselves with "activities"— those who only pray as they are "running around"—but he is afraid of the Christians who are prayer warriors—those who praise, worship, and pray to Almighty God, who go into spiritual warfare clothed in the full armor of God! Andrew Murray, John Wesley, D.L. Moody, and Smith Wigglesworth all said "Prayer takes time, but it is a great time-saver."

Prayer is the key to a fulfilling relationship with God that brings you inner joy, peace, excitement, strength, and contentment. Every day is a new venture with God; you wake up with a spirit of expectation!

I want to emphasize that we <u>are not</u> to make a formula out of prayer. Prayer is communication between you and God. It is you expressing the thoughts that are in your heart and then listening for His answers. Don't be overwhelmed by all the information in this manual. Read through the manual and see what you need to help you grow in your prayer life.

I want to challenge you today to open your life to a life of prayer. You will become stronger and more confident, filled with more love and compassion for mankind than ever before. The world has absolutely nothing to offer you, but a life of prayer with God offers you everything! You meet Him in prayer, and you know you are accepted there.

I have many calls on the prayer line with people asking me to help them with their prayer life. There is no "set" formula for prayer. In this Prayer Manual, I have tried to lay out some basics on subjects I am asked about the most. When you are hungry and thirsty for more of God, take time (in fact, make it <u>top</u> priority) to sit in His presence daily and let the Holy Spirit teach you how to pray. He's just waiting for you to come to Him!

FOREWORD

I believe every ministry ought to have special prayer going up to Heaven so they can fulfill their calling on the earth. Every ministry needs to accomplish and do what God has called them to do. Without prayer, the foundation of any ministry can get very weak and very dim in sight—even lose their vision.

At this time I would like to take this opportunity to thank God for sending to this ministry a real loyal prayer warrior. In my opinion, Ronnie Burch is one of the most dependable and loyal people I have ever known. She has led our early morning prayer time, beginning at 5:00 a.m., in our sanctuary in Cleveland for many years—dependable and faithful every day. Now she is our Prayer Coordinator for our ministry and is one of our teachers in the Bible College. She is also in charge of taking prayer calls in the Prayer Room.

I do appreciate her loyalty in praying for me, and this ministry. It helps keep the presence of God here and makes my ministry easier out on the field. When you have a home team that pulls down strongholds in prayer, God has more avenues to work in.

To close, I again, would like to thank God for sending Ronnie Burch here to this ministry. She is a first class lady, and a first class prayer warrior, who has a precious and sweet spirit that cares for others. We are blessed to have her in Cleveland, and blessed that she has taken the time and effort to share with us her teachings on prayer.

Dr. Norvel Hayes
Founder and President
New Life Bible College & Church

ACKNOWLEDGMENTS

I would like to thank Dr. Norvel Hayes for obeying the voice of God in establishing New Life Bible College. When you come to this college and go through God's "Boot Camp," you receive "new life!"

The first time I heard Brother Norvel teach at the college in 1986, he shared with us how God spoke to him, "Son, the reason My people don't get their prayers answered is that they don't praise and worship Me enough." At this point, he got down on his knees, raised his hands toward Heaven and began praising and worshipping God to demonstrate how he begins each and every day.

Then, in December 1986, someone came to the College and taught on the Blood Covenant. I had heard this taught before, but this time the teaching went into my heart, and I received it as mine. For the first time in my life I knew I was loved—that God loved me because He wanted to love me—that He loved me because He and I are connected by the pure covenant Blood of Jesus. This revelation brought stability and security into my life. I knew I no longer was in bondage, but I was free—free to love others with the God kind of love and there was a burning desire to pray for other people and to see them set free. My prayer for whoever reads or studies this manual is that the Blood Covenant will become a reality in your heart, and that you too will be free to be what God wants you to be!

TABLE OF CONTENTS

LESSON 1
WHY YOU NEED
TO BE SAVED

INTRODUCTION

Before you can enter the kingdom of heaven and know God as your covenant Father, you need to be saved. *For by grace are ye saved through faith; and that not of yourselves: it is the gift of God.* (Ephesians 2:8)

SALVATION

It is God's plan that you be on fire for Him. He wants you healed, delivered, prospering, and set free from any stronghold Satan might try to tie you down with.

But, you will never experience the Spirit of Revival in your life until you are first born again. And, the only way to do that is to accept Jesus as the Son of the living God, and your personal Lord and Savior.

Salvation is the prerequisite to acquiring the fire of God. It is the first step in His plan for a rich and rewarding life. God made a way for that plan to be a reality by sending His only begotten Son to earth to die for the sins of all mankind. Jesus was nailed to the cross so that you and I could be redeemed from the curse, and brought into right standing with the Father.

> Jesus is the only way to God. (1 Timothy 2:4-6)
> Jesus changes us on the inside.
> Jesus wants a relationship with you!

He wants to be your closest friend, one you can rely on in every situation life brings.

God won't force Himself on you. He is just, and will give you the option as to whether you will accept or reject His Son.

The Gospel alone has the power to transform, and it is that Gospel that the unbelieving world desperately needs. The power of the Gospel is sufficient to meet every person's need.

1

Isaiah's name comes from the root meaning of the word "salvation." His name means "Salvation of Jehovah." This is appropriate, since it was he who clearly predicted the saving ministry of Jesus, the suffering servant. (Isaiah 52:13 and 53:11)

Paul, the Apostle, was a Hebrew scholar whose conversion is recorded in Acts 9:1-29. Paul was certain that the Hebrew Law could not change a man's life. He knew the classic thoughts of the Greeks, and the teaching of other cultures. He was willing to take on any philosophy, any ideal, any idea anywhere, at anytime, because he had been undeniably changed and redeemed!

The Gospel has no intellectual or cultural barriers. You do not need a college degree, or reach a certain status in life before Christ will accept you. The power of the Gospel will go inside a man and liberate him. (Luke 4:18)

By accepting Jesus, you will not only gain admittance into Heaven at your death, but you will inherit all the blessings and power God has intended for you to have here on earth. He will replace the old nature with a new one, and all your sins will be washed away, never to be remembered against you anymore.

I.   WHAT THE WORD "SALVATION" MEANS

    A. Webster's Dictionary defines "salvation" as:

        1. A saving or being saved;

        2. A person or thing that saves or rescues;

        3. In theology, the saving of the soul from sin and death, as in Christianity, by the atonement of Jesus.

    B. In the Hebrew language, the word for salvation is "yasha."

        1. To the Hebrews, "yasha" symbolized a deliverance from dangers and narrow straits into restful spaciousness.

        2. This is what happens when you make that important decision to be saved—you are delivered from going

to hell and forgiven of your sins by God's grace. The door is opened for you into God's kingdom, into His rest, His peace, and His joy. You are no longer a sinner; you are a child of God!

3. In Isaiah 12:2 we read, *Behold God is my salvation: I will trust and not be afraid for the Lord JEHOVAH is my strength and my song: He also is become my salvation.*

4. Psalm 34:6 says, *This poor man cried and the Lord heard him, and saved him out of all his troubles.*

C. Humility is the beginning of wisdom. (Proverbs 22:4) You show humility when you come to God and say, "I am a sinner, and I need to be saved."

II. JESUS OUR COVERING

A. When Jesus died at Calvary, He shed His blood for you and me. That blood was then sprinkled on the mercy seat in Heaven.

B. When we accept Jesus as our Lord and Savior, all of our sins (past, present, and future) are forgiven. By being our substitute—by taking our punishment—Jesus became our covering.

C. God has done all that He is going to do in regard to salvation. He gave us the best that He had: *For God so loved the world that He gave His only begotten Son that whosoever believeth in Him should not perish, but have everlasting life. For God sent not His Son into the world to condemn the world, but that the world through Him might be saved.* (John 3:16-17)

III. JESUS OUR RANSOM

A. Before the New Covenant, before Jesus died on the cross, mankind was in bondage to the curse of the law, which is death. *Christ hath redeemed us from the curse of the law, being made a curse for us: for it is written,*

3

cursed is everyone that hangeth on a tree. (Galatians 3:13)

B. Jesus paid it all! He was the ransom needed to set us free from the bondage of the law of sin and death!

IV. THE SINNER'S PRAYER

A. If you are not sure that you are saved, you need to pray the sinner's prayer. This is a very important step—it is the most important decision you will ever make.

B. Please pray the following prayer:

Heavenly Father,

I come to You in the name of Your son, Jesus. I know that I have not lived my life for You. I know that I am a sinner. Today, I turn from sin, I turn away from the lifestyle I have been living, and I repent of my sins. I accept You now, Jesus, into my heart. Your Word says in John 6:37...*and him that cometh to Me, I will in no wise cast out.* I believe Your Word. I believe that You will not turn Your back on me but will receive me into Your kingdom. Thank You for that. Also, Your Word says in Romans 10:9-10, *That if thou shall confess with thy mouth the Lord Jesus, and shalt believe in thine heart that God hath raised Him from the dead, thou shalt be saved. For with the heart man believeth unto righteousness; and with the mouth confession is made unto salvation.*

I believe in my heart that You, Jesus, are the Son of God, and I believe that You were raised from the dead. I confess You now as the Lord of my life. Jesus, thank You, for coming into my heart. I say it now, "I am reborn—I am saved!"

Name:_____

Date:_____

C. The Bible says "thou shalt be saved." It doesn't say you might be saved or you might not be saved. It says you SHALL BE! It is that Word—that promise from God—that guarantees your salvation! Your "feelings" have nothing to do with it. "Feelings" come and go, but God's Word never changes.

V. YOUR PERSONAL EXPERIENCE

If you have received Jesus into your heart, or if you accepted Jesus some time before this, write in your own words what it means to you to have surrendered your life to Jesus.

_____

_____

_____

_____

_____

_____

_____

_____

_____

_____

_____

_____

_____

_____

_____

_____

_____

_____

_____

_____

_____

NOTES

LESSON 2
THE BAPTISM IN
THE HOLY SPIRIT:
WHY YOU NEED IT

INTRODUCTION

After you make Jesus the Lord of your life, it is the will of God that you be filled with His Holy Spirit...*but be filled with the Spirit.* (Ephesians 5:18)

God sent the Holy Spirit on the Day of Pentecost, and the Holy Spirit has been here ever since. It is not up to God to send Him—He is here now. He is the primary agency of the Godhead at work on the earth today. HE IS HERE!

In Luke 24:49, Jesus said, *Tarry ye in Jerusalem....*It was just as necessary for them to be in Jerusalem as it was for them to tarry because, in God's plan, the outpouring of the Holy Spirit had to have its beginning in Jerusalem.

Acts 2:1 says, *And when the day of Pentecost was fully come....* When that came, they didn't have to wait any longer!

In Acts 8:5, 12-17, the Samaritans obviously were saved before the visit of Peter and John. Peter, who ought to know, defined salvation in 1 Peter 1:23 as*, Being born again, not of corruptible seed, but of incorruptible, by the word of God, which liveth and abideth forever.*

They already were saved. The apostles prayed that they might receive the Holy Spirit. Notice this carefully (it will help you help others). Peter and John did not pray that God would **give** the Samaritans the Holy Spirit. *They prayed that they might* **receive** *the Holy Ghost.* We ought to pray according to the Word of God.

It is up to mankind to receive what God offers.

> Eternal life is a gift.
> Healing is a gift.
> The Holy Spirit is a gift.

I. YOUR BODY IS THE TEMPLE OF THE HOLY GHOST

A. Paul said in 1 Corinthians 6:19, *What? know ye not that your body is the temple of the Holy Ghost which is in you....*

B. The Holy Spirit will help you have dominion over the flesh. (Galatians 5:16) As you dwell, habitate, and abide in the Word of God, the Holy Spirit will help you overcome temptation.

When you are baptized with the Holy Ghost, He will give you a burden for the lost.

1. Jesus said, *But ye shall receive power, after that the Holy Ghost is come upon you: and ye shall be witnesses unto Me both in Jerusalem, and in all Judea, and in Samaria, and unto the uttermost part of the earth.* (Acts 1:8)

2. If Jesus' disciples needed that supernatural power to be witnesses for Him here on earth, then we need that power, too!

II. THE GIFT OF THE HOLY GHOST

A. We are told that if we ask for the indwelling of the Holy Spirit, we <u>shall</u> receive.

1. Luke 11:11-13, *If a son shall ask bread of any of you that is a father, will he give him a stone? Or if he ask a fish, will he for a fish give him a serpent?*

v. 12, *or if he shall ask an egg, will he offer him a scorpion?*

v. 13, *If ye then, being evil, know how to give good gifts unto your children: how much more shall your Heavenly Father give the Holy Spirit to them that ask Him?*

B. The following passages show us that being filled with the Holy Spirit is scriptural:

1. Acts 2:1-4, *And when the day of Pentecost was fully come, they were all with one accord in one place.*

   v. 2, *And suddenly there came a sound from heaven as of a rushing mighty wind and it filled all the house where they were sitting.*

   v. 3, *And there appeared unto them cloven tongues like as of fire, and it sat upon each of them.*

   v. 4, *And they were all filled with the Holy Ghost, and began to speak with other tongues, as the Spirit gave them utterance.*

2. Acts 2:38-39, *Then Peter said unto them, Repent, and be baptized every one of you in the name of Jesus Christ for the remission of sins, and ye shall receive the gift of the Holy Ghost.*

   v. 39, *For the promise is unto you, and to your children, and to all that are afar off, even as many as the Lord our God shall call.*

3. Acts 19:1-3, 6, *And it came to pass that while Apollos was at Corinth, Paul having passed through the upper coasts came to Ephesus: and finding certain disciples,*

   v. 2, *He said unto them, Have ye received the Holy Ghost since ye believed? And they said unto him, We have not so much as heard whether there be any Holy Ghost.*

   v. 3, *And he said unto them, Unto what then were ye baptized? And they said, Unto John's baptism.*

   v. 6, *And when Paul had laid his hand upon them, the Holy Ghost came on them: and they spake with tongues, and prophesied.*

C. Other scriptures you may want to read are:

   Luke 24:49   Acts 8:15-17

   John 7:37-39   Acts 9:17-18

John 14:16-17   Acts 10:44-46

Acts 2:32-33   Acts 19:6

Acts 2:38-39   1 Corinthians 14: 2, 18

III. WHY YOU NEED THE BAPTISM OF THE HOLY SPIRIT

A. Listed below are a few of the reasons why you need the baptism in the Holy Spirit:

1. Jesus said you would need this power, supernatural strength, to do His works on earth today. (Acts 1:8)

2. The Baptism in the Holy Spirit:

    a. Edifies and builds up your spirit man. (1 Corinthians 14:4)

    b. Puts you in contact with the deep things of God. (1 Corinthians 2:10)

    c. Allows you to pray the perfect will of God and helps in intercession. (Romans 8:26-27)

3. By speaking in tongues, you speak directly to God, by-passing all human reasoning. (1 Corinthians 14:2)

IV. THE HOLY SPIRIT IS OUR HELPER

A. I have met many beautiful Christians who, through lack of proper teaching, do not even want to talk about the Holy Spirit, much less receive His baptism. It is sad to say that each of these Christians knew they had a call of God on their life, but, due to lack of direction, they remained confused and depressed.

1. This type of Christian actually lives in fear of what the next day will bring, never realizing that it is the devil that is robbing them of their peace, joy, and abundant living. (The traditions of men are robbing Christians of God's blessings.)

2. They look to man for advice instead of spending time on their knees before God until the answer comes. The answer will come if you make God the top priority in your life and spend time before Him in prayer.

B. God invites us to call on Him: *Call unto Me, and I will answer thee, and shew thee great and mighty things, which thou knowest not.* (Jeremiah 33:3)

C. The precious Holy Spirit is the Counselor of all counselors, and He is waiting to help you.

1. God gave the Holy Spirit to Jesus to give to us, His believers, so that we might have power to do His work on the earth today.

2. The Holy Spirit will be your Helper. He knows the mind of God and will direct you every step of the way into God's plans for your life.

3. As you daily yield to His direction, you will receive peace and confidence that only the Holy Spirit can supply.

D. If you are looking for the right mate, pray in the Spirit and be directed by God, for He has the right one for you. Don't lean on your own understanding. (Proverbs 3:5-6) Put your trust and confidence in God, and you will not be fretful or anxious about anything. (Philippians 4:6)

V. THE BAPTISM IN THE HOLY SPIRIT: AN EXPERIENCE APART FROM SALVATION

A. Before we come to the end of this teaching, I would like to answer the question that I have heard many times: "If I don't want to receive my prayer language, will I still go to heaven?" The answer is "yes." If you never speak in tongues, Jesus will love you, and you will still go to heaven if you have been born again by the Spirit of God.

1. To receive or not receive the baptism of the Holy Spirit is a choice that only you can make. It is a free gift from God to give you the power to do the work of Jesus here on earth.

2. Having a prayer language and using it daily in your prayer time builds you up spiritually, strengthening your inner man. It is a beautiful experience that God offers to help us in our walk in the Spirit.

B. The devil has violently attacked this gift; he has distorted and misrepresented its use; he has used this tool to separate families, churches, and the Body of Christ.

1. If people would only stop and think, they would realize that the devil does not want them to have peace, joy, and direction. He does not want them to live in the abundant life that is full of confidence and filled with the things that were bought for them at Calvary by the Blood of Jesus.

2. You received your salvation by the Blood shed at Calvary, and that is only the beginning of all that Jesus' Blood purchased for you.

C. When you are filled with the Holy Spirit, you have spiritual discernment, enabling you to recognize the tactics of the devil. You soon learn how to defeat him and run him out of your life every day.

NOTE: Whether or not you decide to receive the baptism in the Holy Spirit with a heavenly prayer language is entirely up to you. Personally, I want everything Jesus says that I need. He told His disciples to wait until they were endued with power from on high. I want the same supernatural power to do the works of Jesus on the earth today. The choice is yours to accept this gift or reject it.

VI. PRAYER TO RECEIVE THE BAPTISM IN THE HOLY SPIRIT

A. If you desire to receive the baptism in the Holy Spirit with the evidence of speaking in tongues, the Holy

Spirit will give you utterance like He did on the Day of Pentecost.

1. He gives the utterance, but you do the speaking.

2. You need to base your believing on the scriptures that I have listed for you in Section II of this lesson.

3. The Holy Spirit is not an "it." He is a person! He is the Third Person of the Godhead and that is who you are being filled with. (Luke 4:18-19)

B. Receive the baptism in the Holy Spirit by faith as you pray the following prayer:

Dear Heavenly Father,

I have accepted the Lord Jesus as my Lord and Savior. I now come to You and ask You to fill me with Your Holy Spirit and enable me to be a powerful witness for Jesus.

You said in Your Word that if I would ask, I would receive. I ask You now to fill me to overflowing with Your precious Holy Spirit, just as You did the disciples on the Day of Pentecost. I receive Him now by faith and expect to speak with other tongues as He gives me the utterance. Thank You, Father, for blessing me now, in Jesus' Name. Amen.

VII. STEPS IN HELPING PEOPLE RECEIVE THE HOLY SPIRIT

A. Help the person to see that God has already given the Holy Spirit on the Day of Pentecost. It is up to them to receive the gift of the Holy Spirit. The person is not to beg God to fill them with the Holy Spirit. All begging is unbelief.

B. Tell them that anyone who is saved is ready to receive the Holy Spirit. (Acts 2:38)

Some people think that they have to clean up their lives before they receive the Holy Spirit. But, if they are saved, they have the Blood of Jesus, and they're Blood washed and Blood bought.

C. It is scriptural to tell people to expect to receive the Holy Spirit when hands are laid on them.

D. Tell the person what to expect: expect the Spirit to move on their vocal cords and put supernatural words on their lips. The Holy Spirit gives the utterance, but man does the speaking. Acts 2:4 says, *And they were all filled with the Holy Ghost....*

Acts 10:46
1 Corinthians 14:2
1 Corinthians 14:18

E. Tell the person to throw away all fear he picked up from foolish teachers, that he might receive something false. Help him to see that he will not receive a substitute for the Holy Spirit. (Luke 11:11-13)

F. Encourage the person to open his mouth and tell God, "I am receiving the Holy Spirit right now by faith." Encourage them not to speak in their natural language.

G. Don't crowd around persons who come seeking the infilling of the Spirit. Don't give them confusing instructions.

VIII. YOUR PERSONAL EXPERIENCE

A. If you prayed today to receive the baptism of the Holy Spirit with the evidence of speaking in tongues, you need to write down what happened—tell how God touched your life today.

NOTES

LESSON 3
WHO IS THE HOLY SPIRIT?

INTRODUCTION

Each time I attempted to write about the Holy Spirit, such a spirit of humility and brokenness swept over me that I questioned: "How can I ever put into words the preciousness of His companionship?" He is so gentle, so loving, so caring, so kind, and yet, all powerful! He is always ready to help us in any situation that we may face, but we have to ask for His help. He wants to be our constant companion. The Holy Spirit reveals Jesus to us. He helps us to see Jesus so clearly.

We are taught when we are saved who God is and who Jesus is. We are taught that we need to be baptized in the Holy Spirit with the initial evidence of speaking in tongues. However, the teaching usually ends there. Very little is taught about the Holy Spirit Himself. He comes to live within us and to help us in every area of our lives so that we might live victoriously! Because the Holy Spirit is a gift from God, we can choose to receive Him or to reject Him.

Today we are living in a time of revival of the Holy Spirit. We must get to know the Holy Spirit so that we will understand (in the Spirit) what is happening. How do we do this? By entering into a life of prayer, we become aware of His nature and of how very much He desires to fellowship with us. My prayer is that the Holy Spirit will become a reality to anyone who reads this manual. He will give you joy, peace, security, and confidence that you have never known.

The Spirit of God is not just in heaven. He is here in the earth. He is in all of us! (John 4:14) He is our Advocate here on earth. Jesus is our Advocate in Heaven. The Holy Spirit wants to impart Heaven to you! He does not want you sick or suffering. He wants you to drink from the fountain of life.

The Holy Spirit will help you in a relationship—help you not to want everything done your way. You just cannot lose with the Holy Spirit inside you, and the surrounding angels keeping you from stumbling. The Holy Spirit shows us how to tune our hearts to the heart of the Father. The Holy Spirit is the eternal life of God living on the inside of us!

God has raised up a people who will know the life and ministry of the Holy Spirit more than any before us. What God is doing on the earth today will pass right by you if you are not listening to the Holy Spirit.

Meditation in the Word brings your spirit and your mind together and builds your capacity for faith! It also makes you very sensitive to the leadership of the Holy Spirit! The Holy Spirit knows what you and I need and how to get it done. Do things His way—it works!

The early Christians were totally dependent upon the Holy Spirit. They were open channels through which the power of God could flow freely. (1 Corinthians 2:4-5)

The Holy Spirit is preparing you for your future. Your obedience to the Holy Spirit <u>NOW</u> will make the difference later! Be prepared to build your life around the blueprint of God. God has called you to things bigger than you are, and He's called people to help you. These are divine and glorious connections that He has made.

This is absolutely the greatest hour to be alive!

I. **THE HOLY SPIRIT IS A PERSON**

    A. In the Hebrew, "Holy Spirit" or "Holy Ghost" means "holy breath" or "the breath that is holy." The Holy Spirit is the breath of God touching our lives. God's life is in His breath!

    B. Why is the Holy Spirit here?

       1. To Help. (Romans 8:26)

       2. To Teach. (John 16:13)

       3. To Reveal. (Galatians 1:16, 1 John 2:27)

4. To Empower. (Acts 1:8, 2 Corinthians 10:4, Ephesians 3:16, Colossians 1:11)

C. John 14:26 (Amplified Bible) *But the Comforter (Counselor, Helper, Intercessor, Advocate, Strengthener, Standby), the Holy Spirit, whom the Father will send in My Name (in My place, to represent Me and act on My behalf), He will teach you all things. He will teach you whatever you need to know. And He will cause you to recall (will remind you of, bring to your remembrance) everything I have told you.*(See 1 John 2:27.)

D. In the Greek, the word "comforter" denotes capability, or one adapted for giving aid. The Holy Spirit brings peace that the world knows nothing about. The Holy Spirit is fully able to assist us in life. God wants us to talk with the Holy Spirit all day long—not just when we're praying.

E. In 2 Corinthians 13:14, Paul speaks of the communion we are to have with the Holy Ghost, *The grace of the Lord Jesus Christ, and the love of God and the communion of the Holy Ghost, be with you all.*

II. THE POWER OF THE HOLY SPIRIT

A. As believers, we need to realize that the Holy Spirit is powerful. His power lives within us, ready to be released when we totally yield to Him daily.

B. God sent the Holy Ghost to live in us, to give us the power to live victorious lives. The Holy Spirit gives us power for service. Jesus told His disciples in Acts 1:8, *But, ye shall receive power, after that the Holy Ghost is come upon you: and ye shall be witnesses unto Me in Jerusalem, and in all Judea, and in Samaria, and unto the uttermost part of the earth.*

C. John 15:4, *Abide in Me, and I in you. As the branch cannot bear fruit of itself, except it abide in the vine; no more can ye, except ye abide in Me.*

19

1. The Hebrew word for "abide" is "gur." This means "to turn aside from one's own way to some person or place with the idea of lodging there."

2. The happiest person in the world is one who turns from his own way and abides with Him who is "The Way."

3. As we yield to the Holy Spirit, He will guide our lives. As we surrender daily to the Holy Spirit, we place ourselves under the Lord's care and protection.

D. We must not ignore the Holy Spirit: *And grieve not the Holy Spirit of God, whereby ye are sealed unto the day of redemption.* (Ephesians 4:30)

1. When we invite the Holy Spirit into our lives— we fellowship with Him and daily welcome His direction and guidance—He becomes all that we need Him to be. However, when we ignore Him, the Holy Spirit is grieved. He is a gentleman; He does not come where He is not wanted.

2. We cannot lose the infilling of the Holy Spirit immediately. The Holy Spirit only leaves when He is repeatedly (continuously) ignored. He is patient. He sees beyond our occasional failures to our heart and what we will become or do for God.

III. ATTRIBUTES OF THE HOLY SPIRIT

A. The Holy Spirit is a Person.

1. To get to know the Holy Spirit, we must spend time communing with Him in prayer. He longs to fellowship with us, and He wants to talk with us throughout the day.

2. The Holy Spirit wants to give us life and peace, *For to be carnally minded is death; but to be spiritually minded is life and peace.* (Romans 8:6)

B. He is the third person of the Trinity. (1 John 5:7)

C. The Holy Ghost is the Voice of God. (Hebrews 3:7)

D. The Holy Spirit has the Mind of God—He thinks just as God thinks. (Romans 8:14, 27, 1 Corinthians 2:12-13, 16)

E. The Holy Spirit is symbolized by the dove. The Holy Spirit is gentle (like a dove) and yet all powerful. (Matthew 3:16)

F. The Holy Spirit is our personal Intercessor. He is specific in His intercession because His intercession is according to the will of God. Because He has the mind of the Father, He can intervene to keep us from praying wrong prayers. (Romans 8:26-27)

When you feel inadequate to pray or, you are not happy with your prayer life, it is because you are trying to build a prayer life in your own strength. Ask the Holy Spirit to help you develop your prayer life.

G. The Holy Spirit is our Counselor. We need to cease running from person to person for counseling. Just be still and spend time with the Holy Spirit: let the Counselor of all counselors—the divine Counselor, the Holy Spirit—be your Counselor. (John 14:26, Amplified Bible)

NOTE: One observation I have made is that people who constantly need counseling have a very shallow prayer life and lack stability in their lives. A strong prayer life will give you stability in every area of your life and will build strong character in you. Every Christian has the Spirit of God in him or her, and needs to be led by the inward witness. Ask the Holy Spirit to help you develop your prayer life.

H. The Holy Spirit is our Comforter. (John 14:16, 26)

I. The Holy Spirit is the Spirit of Truth. (John 15:26; John 16:13, 1 John 4:6; 5:6) The Holy Spirit reveals Jesus to us.

J. The Holy Spirit gives Life. (John 6:63, Romans 8:1, 2 Corinthians 3:6, 1 Peter 3:18)

K. The Holy Spirit is our Strengthener. (John 14:26 Amplified Bible)

L. The Holy Spirit is our Teacher. Ask Him to help you read the Bible.

   1. The Holy Spirit will impart to us revelation knowledge about the scriptures. He will quicken that Word to our spirit. (Psalm 119:50) We need to understand that only by the Spirit living in us, and yielding ourselves to Him, will we be able to understand the Word of God.

   2. He teaches us how to "abide." When you "abide," you dwell there on a continual basis. He shows us how to please God and how to remain in God's anointing. He is a living communion between God and man. (We do not forget Jesus when we fellowship with the Holy Spirit. Jesus gave us the Holy Spirit! The Holy Spirit is the One who glorifies Jesus!)

   3. We should let the Holy Spirit teach us. (Luke 12:12, John 14:26, 1 Corinthians 2:13, 1 John 2:20, 27)

M. The Holy Spirit is our divine Helper.

   1. The Holy Spirit helps us love God more. (Romans 5:5)

   2. The Holy Spirit helps us pray. (Jude 20)

   3. The Holy Spirit helps us worship God. (John 4:24, Philippians 3:3)

   4. The Holy Spirit helps us wait on God. (Galatians 5:5)

   5. The Holy Spirit helps us have dominion over our flesh. If we live in oneness with the Holy Ghost, the flesh will not have dominion over us. (Galatians 5:16)

   6. The Holy Spirit helps us to be free from bondage.

    a. When we are yielding our lives to the Holy Spirit, then there is liberty.

    b. Christians should not be in bondage to any living person or thing! We should be free in the Spirit, *Now the Lord is that Spirit and where the Spirit of the Lord is, there is liberty.* (2 Corinthians 3:17)

N. The Holy Spirit anoints us to preach and teach the Word of God with power and authority. (Acts 1:8; 7:54-56; 18:9-10; 28:30-31)

O. The Holy Spirit will help us develop childlike characteristics.

    1. A child is trusting, humble, and teachable. These characteristics are directly opposite of the world's way of thinking, but these characteristics are pleasing unto God.

    2. Matthew 18:2-4, *And Jesus called a little child unto Him, and set him in the midst of them.*

    v. 3, *And said, Verily I say to you, Except ye be converted, and become as little children, ye shall not enter into the kingdom of heaven.*

    v. 4, *Whosoever therefore shall humble himself as this little child, the same is greatest in the kingdom of heaven.*

P. The Holy Spirit guides us by speaking to our spirit man. (Romans 8:14, 16)

NOTES

LESSON 4
LIVING A LIFE OF PRAYER

PART ONE: COMMUNICATION WITH GOD

INTRODUCTION

We need to practice the presence of God every day in everything we do. Hold on to your place in the Spirit. It seems to me we have made prayer more complicated than it is. It is communication with God. Max Lucado says, "Anchor deep, say a prayer and hold on. Don't be surprised if someone walks across the water to give you a hand." (Hebrews 6:19)

Isaiah 56:7 says, *"My house will be called a house of prayer."* We are God's house of prayer. 1 Corinthians 3:16 says, *"know ye not that ye are the temple of God, and that the Spirit of God dwelleth in you?"*

In the Old Testament (or the Old Covenant), God's house was a temple built in HIS honor. Today, we are under the New Covenant and God no longer lives in a temple of stone but in our spirits when we are born again.

We want to be careful that we do not make a "formula" from the way someone else prays!

I. FELLOWSHIP WITH THE FATHER

A. Fellowshipping with the Father is the foundation of powerful prayer.

1. Come before Him first of all with thanksgiving, praise, and worship. That is why it is so important that we pray for revelation knowledge concerning the Blood Covenant—the Covenant the Father has provided for us to be in Covenant with Him. As we spend time in His presence, (1 Corinthians 13 AMP) will become easier and easier! He provided this Covenant so that we may know, beyond a shadow of a doubt, that by Jesus' sacrifice and His

Blood, we have access to the throne room of God as we praise Him.

2. It is God's fellowship (His presence) that makes prayer a delight.

II. PRAYING FROM YOUR HEART

A. Scriptures: 1 Samuel 1:13 (Hannah); 10:9; 16:7, Psalms 51:17, Proverbs 3:5.

B. Pray for all in authority first of all.

1. After we have been in His presence praising and worshipping, then we need to pray for all authority figures (1 Timothy 2:1-2) before we pray for ourselves and our families. *I exhort therefore, that, first of all, supplications, prayers, intercessions, and giving of thanks, be made for all men; For kings; and for all that are in authority; that we may lead a quiet and peaceable life in all godliness and honesty.*

C. Be sensitive to the heartbeat of the Father.

1. When we have been fellowshipping with our Father, we are sensitive to His heartbeat, so we pray in that direction, guided by the inner ear of our heart.

2. The Holy Spirit dwelling inside you and me helps us to be sensitive to God's desires and helps us to be obedient to His desires.

3. Having a quality prayer life will give you peace in your mind instead of confusion. (Isaiah 26:3)

III. LEARNING TO BE SENSITIVE TO THE HOLY SPIRIT

A The Holy Spirit will teach you when to ask for His help.

1. According to John 14:26, God does not want prayer to be a rigid formula, or dry and laborious. He wants us to learn to pray from our hearts.

2. 1 John 2:27, *But the anointing which ye have received of God abideth in you and ye need not that any man teach you: but as the same anointing teacheth you of all things, and is truth, and is no lie, and even as it hath taught you, ye shall abide in Him.*

3. Be sure you have a "heart check-up" daily because this is where the Holy Spirit dwells, and you don't want anything there to keep you from hearing Him and obeying Him. Prayers that really count come from your heart—not your head. (Proverbs 4:20-23)

IV. DAILY TIME IN THE WORD

A. You need to spend time daily in the Word of God.

1. People who feed on the Word of God find it's easier for them to follow their heart. Transfer the scriptures from your head to your heart. God's Word is essential to our prayer lives. We need to stop and refuel on His Word so our prayers will have more power.

2. The Golden Rule of Prayer: John 15:7.

3. Be consistent! (John 6:63, Hebrews 1:3)

4. When we faithfully read the Word of God and act on His Word, and we are consistent in our prayer lives, that is when the power of God will operate in our lives.

V. ACCURACY IN PRAYER

A. Always base your prayer request on scripture.

1. Find your scripture for your situation, and remind God of His Word, and of His promises. (Isaiah 43:26)

2. Believe you receive when you pray! (Matthew 21:21-22)

VI. CONCLUSION

We also need to spend time reading and meditating on the Word of God. The more we do this, the easier it will be for us to tell whether or not the promptings are from God. You will be able to discern the difference between your mind and your heart, because the Word will help you divide the two.

It's <u>not</u> a formula, but God's <u>presence</u>, that makes prayer a delight and keeps our prayers on the right course! Prayer keeps you refreshed! You want your communion to flow from your heart to God.

Praying by the unction of the Holy Spirit is the only Biblical way to pray. Don't try to copy the way someone else prays. Learn to follow the leading of the Holy Spirit so your prayer life will be exciting! (Romans 8:14)

In John 7:38-39, Jesus said, *He that believeth on Me, as the scripture hath said, out of his belly shall flow rivers of living water.* Jesus said "rivers" would flow from us, not just one river! Those rivers include all kinds of prayer. When you let the river of the Spirit flow, you'll not only go in the right direction, you'll begin to go deeper into the realms of the Spirit.

In Ezekiel 47:1-5, the prophet, Ezekiel, had a vision of those deeper waters:

Afterward he brought me again unto the door of the house; and, behold, waters issued out from under the threshold of the house eastward: for the forefront of the house stood toward the east, and the waters came down from under the right side of the house, at the south side of the altar. Then brought he me out of the way of the gate northward, and led me about the way without unto the utter gate by the way that looketh eastward; and behold there ran out waters on the right side. And when the man that had the line in his hand went forth eastward, he measured a thousand cubits, and he brought me through the waters; the waters were to the ankles. Again he measured a thousand cubits,

28

and brought me through the waters; the waters were to the knees. Again he measured a thousand, and brought me through; the waters were to the loins. Afterward he measured a thousand; and it was a river that I could not pass over: for the waters were risen, waters to swim in, a river that could not be passed over.

That is the way Spirit-led prayer progresses. God doesn't throw you out in the deep waters when you first begin praying, any more than you would put a child who was just learning to swim in the middle of a river. No, He starts you off in ankle deep water. Then, as you begin to grow in faith and learn to flow with Him, He will take you into those knee deep waters.

The more you cultivate your relationship with Him through prayer and the Word, the more your anointing for prayer will increase. You will soon find yourself moving into places in prayer you never could have imagined when your first began.

Simply seek the Lord Himself. Spend time in His Word and in prayer every day. Then, follow Him and yield to the promptings He puts in your heart. You'll never be able to pray the right kind of prayer directed by head-knowledge, because the Bible says, *We know not what we should pray for as we ought!* (Romans 8:26)

NOTES

LESSON 4
LIVING A LIFE OF PRAYER

PART TWO: PRAYER—THE SOURCE

Foundation Scriptures: **Isaiah 59:1**
                             1 John 3:22; 4:17-18
                             Luke 18:1

I. THE BELIEVER HAS WEAPONS THAT GUARANTEE RESULTS IN PRAYER (Ephesians 6:10-18)

A. The Name of Jesus.

B. The Word of God. (John 15:7, 2 Peter 1:2-4)

C. The power of the Holy Spirit. (Romans 8:26-29)

D. Living a life of thanksgiving, praise, and worship.

E. Getting dressed daily in the whole armor of God.

II. LET HIM ASK IN FAITH— NOTHING WAVERING (James 1:6-8)

A. God will hear you! (Romans 4:16)

III. PRAYER IS THE FOUNDATION OF EVERY CHRISTIAN ENDEAVOR (John 15:7, Colossians 1:10, Hebrews 13:21)

A. Regardless of any man's ability, he will ultimately fail if not backed by prayer.

B. Failure of all Christian enterprises is a prayer failure or not being obedient to do what God tells you to do in a time of prayer!

IV. STEPS TO A DEEPER LIFE IN PRAYER

A. Always come into His presence with thanksgiving: (praise and worship).

1. Ask the Father in Jesus' name (John 16:23), not for Jesus' sake.

2. Believe that you receive. (Matthew 21:22, Mark 11:24)

3. When you stand praying, forgive. (Mark 11:25)

4. Depend on the Holy Spirit to help in prayer. (Romans 8:26, 1 Corinthians 14:14)

5. Pray the prayer of intercession. (1 Timothy 2:1)

6. Take time to pray in the Spirit to build yourself up. (1 Corinthians 14:14, Jude 20)

7. When you pray in the Spirit, pray to interpret. (1 Corinthians 14:13)

B. Prayer based on the Word is prayer based on the Lord's will.

1. Jeremiah 1:12.

2. 1 John 3:22; 5:14-15.

3. 1 Timothy 2:1: Prayer needs to precede counseling, committee meetings, witnessing, etc.

4. Romans 8:26: We are to turn to the Holy Spirit for help. He will help us pray effectively.

V. CONCLUSION

You and I can read all the scriptures and make all the right confessions, but if we are not walking in love and forgiveness, our prayers will not be answered. God looks on our hearts, not on the outside!

NOTES

LESSON 5
GOD'S COVENANT
WITH MAN

INTRODUCTION

In this lesson, we will study some of the things God has provided for us under the New Covenant. We are to walk not only in the blessings of Abraham but also in a preferred chain of blessings because of the Blood of Jesus that was shed for us at Calvary. We need to carefully study this lesson, get it down in our hearts, and start walking and living like God's covenant children.

Once you are born again, you belong to God's family. You have entered into your covenant with God. He is your covenant Father, and you are His covenant child. All that He has belongs to you, and all that you have belongs to Him—that is "covenant" talk!

Saints of God, <u>every time</u> God cuts covenant, it's because of love and friendship. Every time God had a friend, He cut a covenant with him. Why? Because God wanted to love that man, protect that man, and take care of that man and his family. But, God cannot make a covenant with you if you are a rebel!

Don't settle for less, when you can have all that God has promised. God wants to make you whole in every area of your life!

Deliverance from sin is just the beginning of your salvation. Once you have accepted Jesus into your heart, you are entitled to:

1. Freedom from sin.
2. Protection from danger.
3. Deliverance.
4. Supernatural guidance.

I. OUR COVENANT RIGHTS

A. Once you have made Jesus Christ the Lord of your life, your spirit man is literally born again. *Therefore if any man be in Christ, he is a new creature: old things are passed away; behold, all things are become new.* (2 Corinthians 5:17)

B. Most Christians do not even know that they have covenant rights simply because Satan has tried to blind us—tried to keep us from walking a victorious walk—he has tried to keep us under the curse of the law, but we have been redeemed from the curse of the law. Galatians 3:13-14, 26-29 states:

v. 13, *Christ hath redeemed us from the curse of the law being made a curse for us: for it is written, Cursed is everyone that hangeth on a tree.*

v. 14, *That the blessing of Abraham might come on the Gentiles through Jesus Christ; that we might receive the promise of the Spirit through faith.*

v. 26, For *ye are all the children of God by faith in Christ Jesus.*

v. 27, *For as many of you as have been baptized into Christ have put on Christ.*

v. 28, *There is neither Jew nor Greek, there is neither bond nor free, there is neither male nor female: for ye are all one in Christ Jesus.*

v. 29, *And if ye be Christ's, then are ye Abraham's seed, and heirs according to the promise.*

C. Genesis 17:1-7, 9

v. 1, *And when Abram was ninety years old and nine, the Lord appeared to Abram, and said unto him, I am the Almighty God; walk before Me, and be thou perfect.*

v. 2, *And I will make My covenant between Me and thee, and I will multiply thee exceedingly.*

v. 3, *And Abram fell on his face: and God talked with him, saying*

v. 4, *As for Me, behold, My covenant is with thee, and thou shalt be a father of many nations.*

v. 5, *Neither shall thy name any more be called Abram but thy name shall be Abraham; for a father of many nations have I made thee.*

v. 6, *And I will make thee exceeding fruitful, and I will make nations of thee, and kings shall come out of thee.*

v. 7, *And I will establish My covenant between Me and thee and thy seed after thee in their generations for an everlasting covenant, to be a God unto thee, and to thy seed after thee.*

v. 9, *And God said unto Abraham, Thou shall keep My covenant therefore, thou, and thy seed after thee in their generations.*

D. In verse seven God said "I will establish." God says to you and to me that the Covenant He established (fixed or set) with Abraham is a promise that cannot be altered. The promises of the covenant are guaranteed by God. No enemy could successfully stand before Abraham because he had a covenant with God, and the same is true for you and me!

E. Genesis 15:18-21

v. 18, *In the same day the Lord made a covenant with Abram, saying, Unto they seed have I given this land, from the river of Egypt unto the great river, the river Euphrates.*

v. 19, *The Kenites, and the Kenizzites, and the Kadmonites,*

v. 20, *And the Hittites, and the Perizzites, and the Rephaims,*

v. 21, *And the Amorites, and the Canaanites, and the Girgashites, and the Jebusites.*

The very fact of Israel's existence is because of the Abrahamic Covenant. The very miracles of God performed in Egypt were promises made to Abraham. God will never go back on His promises!

F. Galatians 3:29 says that we are *heirs according to the promise*. We are both seeds and heirs. God has obligated Himself to bless us as He blessed Abraham. The promise to us is that God will establish His covenant with us NOW, in this generation!

G. In Deuteronomy 28, God spelled out the blessings of Abraham. As the seed of Abraham, you are to receive everything that is yours by Christ Jesus, as a glory to God. You can expect God to move because of His covenant with you—not when you get to Heaven, but NOW!

II. BLESSED WITH GIFTS OF THE HOLY SPIRIT

A. Do you see how far short we have been walking when our covenant Father has provided everything by the Blood of Calvary for us to walk under the New Covenant? Once we are born again, we ask and receive the fullness of the Holy Spirit. When we receive the Holy Spirit, we are blessed with the gifts of the Holy Spirit, and we receive the ability of God.

B. Jesus said the Holy Spirit would teach us all things. (John 14:26) You as a member of the Body—a partaker of your covenant with God—must individually receive that which He has already given. He has been sent to you.

III. MADE TO BE IN RIGHT-STANDING WITH GOD

A. As a covenant child of your covenant Father, you have been put in right-standing with God. The covenant between Jesus and God is signed in the Blood of the Lamb, and provides that you are in right-standing with God. You have a right to every single thing that God has.

B. Righteousness becomes a driving force, a security force, which will rise up within you and cause you to meet Satan face-to-face.

C. Whatever your situation, you must believe that you have been made to be in right-standing with God, and that you can come <u>boldly</u> into the Throne Room of grace to obtain mercy and to find grace and help in time of need. (Hebrews 4:16)

IV. HEALING BELONGS TO US

A. As a covenant child of your covenant Father, you have a right to divine health. It is one of your covenant rights. The problem has been that most Christians do not know that healing *belongs* to them.

B. Healing was not introduced during the ministry of Jesus, nor is it only a New Covenant blessing. God has always provided healing for His people through His covenants. In Exodus 15:26, He said, *For I am the Lord that healeth thee.* He placed Himself as Israel's healer—Jehovah Rapha. God never changes!

C. Jesus bore your sins on the cross, and He bore your disease, weakness, and pain as well. Satan will still try to put these things on you, but you resist him—they do not belong to you. James 4:7 says, *Submit yourselves therefore to God. Resist the devil, and he will flee from you.*

D. We, as God's people, should develop faith concerning healing as highly as we have developed it for salvation. Your healing was purchased 2,000 years ago by the sacrifice of Jesus: *Surely He (Jesus) hath borne our griefs, and carried our sorrows: yet we did esteem Him stricken, smitten of God, and afflicted.*

v. 5, *But He was wounded for our transgressions, He was bruised for our iniquities: the chastisement of our peace was upon Him; and with His stripes we were healed.* (Isaiah 53:4-5)

E. Jesus was smitten of God with sin and sickness in order for you to go free. When Jesus bore away our sins, He also bore away our diseases. The cross pronounced a double cure for the ills of mankind.

F. We are covenant people, and we have been made as free from sickness as we have from sin. We need to make the decision to walk in divine health in the same way we made the decision to accept Jesus as Savior.

V. ANGELS

A. For the most part, we as born again Christians (heirs of the promise) have not been using the angel power that is available to us. God is able and mighty to perform His Word: *Are they not all ministering spirits, sent forth to minister for them who shall be heirs of salvation?* (Hebrews 1:14)

B. The angels of God have been sent to minister for the heirs of the promise of Abraham. (Genesis 17) They have been sent to perform whatever is necessary to establish God's promise in the earth! The angels are assigned to administer, or enforce, the blessings of Abraham to His seed in the current generation.

C. Just as surely as God established His covenant with Isaac, He is obligated by His own Word to establish His covenant with you. We have already discussed the fact that if you have made Jesus the Lord of your life, then you are the seed of Abraham and heir to His blessings. (Galatians 3:29)

From Genesis to Revelation you read about the angels administering God's covenant to Abraham and his seed. The angels are to administer the New Covenant (which is the fulfillment of the Old Covenant) to the heirs of promise.

D. When you confess the Word of God over a situation, you put your angels to work. You have angels assigned to you. The words of your mouth bind them or loose them to work for you. If you speak faith-filled words enforced by God's Word, your angels are free to bring about what you want to come to pass. Watch the words that come out of your mouth!

VI. PROSPERITY BELONGS TO US

A. The Christian who stays in poverty rejects the establishment of the covenant. *Beloved, I wish* [pray] *above all things that thou mayest prosper and be in health, even as thy soul prospereth.* (3 John 2)

B. God cannot establish His covenant in your life without prospering you. The covenant cannot be established in your life unless you believe God's Word concerning prosperity. God's will is to establish His covenant in the earth: *But you shall remember the Lord your God; for it is He who gives you power to get wealth, that He may establish His covenant which He swore to your fathers, as at this day* (Deuteronomy 8:18, Amplified Bible.) "As at this day" is as though He made the agreement with you today!

C. Just think how much easier the laws of prosperity will work for us under the New Covenant. We have all the blessings of the Old Covenant plus the power (the Blood shed at Calvary) of the New. We have been born again, and we have the nature of God. We are one spirit with the Lord. Jesus has recovered the authority Adam lost.

D. We are the seed of Abraham in this generation, and enjoy the promise of spiritual deliverance. Satan has been defeated and put under our feet! God is still God. All through the Bible, God proves that He will go to any length to establish His covenant with Abraham and his seed (Romans 8:32). He is the covenant-keeping God in our generation. *My covenant will I not break: nor alter the thing that is gone out of My lips.* (Psalm 89:34)

VII. BECAUSE OF GOD'S COVENANT WITH MAN, WE HAVE AUTHORITY OVER SATAN AND DEMONS

A. We have already established the fact that once you have made Jesus the Lord of your life, and received the infilling of the Holy Spirit, you are a new creation in right-standing with God. You are an heir of God—a joint heir with Jesus—enjoying your covenant blessings. (Romans 8:17) Because of your covenant, you have authority over Satan and his demons.

B. The authority Adam gave Satan when Adam sinned was seized by Jesus at His death and resurrection. Jesus conquered Satan in his own domain: *And having spoiled principalities and powers, He made a shew of them openly, triumphing over them in it.* (Colossians 2:15) In other words, Jesus paralyzed Satan; he has been disarmed (no weapons) where God's covenant people are concerned.

C. All the power and authority Satan uses in the earth now belongs to the church of Jesus Christ. Satan is using our own authority against us through deception.

D. Because of your covenant with God, you have authority over all beings—in heaven, in earth, and under the earth. You are given the right to use the Name of Jesus when you receive Him as Lord. (Philippians 2:9-11)

E. Ephesians 6:12 says, *For we wrestle not against flesh and blood but against principalities. Against powers, against the rulers of the darkness of this world, against spiritual wickedness in high places.*

In the world of the Spirit, there is a counterfeit, an opponent to God. Satan and his evil forces are determined to ruin everything you do for God so that it will all end in failure. But you have been given the armor of God to stand against the devil and his forces.

F. Satan is no match for the believer who attacks the source with the full armor of God, and no longer struggles against the problems of life. We must be obedient to the Word of God, and put on His full armor every day, just as we put on our clothes. (Ephesians 6:10-18)

G. Isaiah 54:17 says, *No weapon that is formed against thee shall prosper; and every tongue that shall rise against thee in judgment thou shalt condemn. This is the heritage of the servants of the Lord, and their righteousness is of Me, saith the Lord.*

H. Matthew 28:18-20, *And Jesus came and spake unto them, saying, All power is given unto Me in heaven and in earth.*

v. 19, *Go ye therefore, and teach all nations, baptizing them in the Name of the Father, and of the Son, and of the Holy Ghost.*

v. 20, *Teaching them to observe all things whatsoever I have commanded you: and, lo, I am with you alway, even unto the end of the world.*

Mark 16:17-18, *And these signs shall follow them that believe; In My name shall they cast out devils; they shall speak with new tongues;*

v. 18, *They shall take up serpents; and if they drink any deadly thing, it shall not hurt them; they shall lay hands on the sick, and they shall recover.*

VIII. CONCLUSION

In Genesis 15, God cut covenant with Abram. In Deuteronomy 28:1-4, God renewed the Abrahamic Covenant with Moses. There were blessings and curses in the Old Covenant.

Although we have been guilty of breaking the terms of the covenant, we have been freed from the penalty of it. The Body of Christ needs to come into the fullness of the covenant!

We need to hold on and possess what the New Covenant gives us. (Galatians 3:16, 29) Romans 8:17 calls us "joint-heirs with Jesus Christ." Through the New Covenant, God has promised to care for us the same way He would love and care for Jesus!

NOTES

LESSON 6
THE BLOOD COVENANT

INTRODUCTION

Many people have asked me this question: WHAT IS PLEADING THE BLOOD OF JESUS? And then they will say, I want to be excited about the Blood Covenant, but I just don't understand it!

ANSWER: God sees us through Calvary. Whenever you plead the blood, you come into the presence of God, and are tapping into the resources of the Almighty. When facing a difficulty, I plead the Blood of Jesus Christ, and take it even further: "The Lord Jesus Christ, who died on Calvary for the sins of the whole world, by whose Blood I am made clean, and by whose Blood I have protection over all the forces of the enemy, I plead for that protection to come now, and I rebuke you, Satan, by the Blood of Jesus!" It works!

For many years I had been pleading the Blood of Jesus over myself, my home, and my family members. Then Billye Brim came to New Life Bible Church and taught us to say this every time we get into our cars. "I plead the Blood of Jesus inside and outside, front to back, side to side over this vehicle, and I declare and decree I will not bump anyone and no one will bump me." It works!

The word "hesed" is the Hebrew word for "mercy" and it means mercy, loving kindness, and fidelity. "Hesed" (or mercy and loving kindness) is the very nature of God.

The Blood Covenant is the unconditional love of God for you and me. Once you accept Jesus as your Savior, you get in on His Blood Covenant with the Father. Our Father God, in His unconditional love for you and me, wants to love us, protect us, and provide for us.

Once we understand and receive His love and protection, then we dare to drop the walls we have built up trying not to be hurt anymore—we let the wounds heal quicker and reach out to

45

others to walk in the God kind of love and forgiveness with our family and friends.

All of a sudden, you have a burning desire to "give," to win souls, to look for someone you can be a blessing to on a daily basis. You are taking on the characteristics of God! The heart of our Covenant Father is to "give" to us—to be a blessing to us. He desires for us to walk in the fullness of all that He has already provided. The enemy does not want us to know about the Blood Covenant. The devil wants us bound with a "sack full" of unforgiveness. Every time someone hurts our feelings, we just open up this "sack" we've been carrying around and shove in another hurt or grudge so we can be sure we don't forget what someone said or did to us.

But once you become "covenant minded," you no longer think that way, but remind yourself of the promises of God in His word that you are free according to Isaiah 10:27, Mark 2:22-26, 2 Corinthians 3: 17, Galatians 3:13-14, 29 (the anointing has "yoke" destroying power).

God has so much more for us than we ever dreamed possible when we make a quality decision to be quick to repent and to walk in love and forgiveness!

Once you start meditating about the Blood Covenant and what it means, every time you pick up the Bible, you will read a scripture and immediately you'll say, "That's covenant talk— that's the hesed-agape love of God!"

Example:

Psalm 23, Psalm 103, Psalm 136, Hebrews 13:5, and many more scriptures.

The Father-heart of God longed for sons and daughters. This yearning passion took form, and God planned to create a man who would walk with Him as His child.

Ephesians 1:4-5: *According as He made choice of us in Him before the foundings of the world, that we might be holy and blameless in His presence. In love marking us out beforehand unto Sonship through Jesus Christ for Himself.*

Before God created a world—in His dream plan—man was marked out for Sonship. He was to hold the place of the son in the Father God's love. He was to be the answer to the Father's hunger for children.

Knowing that fellowship is the reason for man, we can understand that man could not meet the reason for his very existence unless he was created in God's image. (Genesis 1:26)

THE BLOOD COVENANT IS
A COVENANT OF GOD'S LOVE (John 3:16)

God refuses to cease to love. "Agape" means covenant love. I choose to honor the Blood of Jesus, because God honors the Blood. Covenant is a sign of God's love and protection.

The purpose of covenant is to establish an unbreakable relationship. The word "covenant" is used more than 280 times in the Bible. God is a covenant God. He believes in covenant, and operates in covenant (Deuteronomy 7:9). God mentions "the Blood" over 700 times in the Bible. If it is that important to God, we would do well to learn all we can about the Blood. For thousands of years, God has been working to drop the revelation of His love into the hearts of men. He's made loving promises of blessings and protection. But He has always faced that same obstacle—human beings who just couldn't bring themselves to believe those promises were true. It just seems too good to be true!

COVENANT IS STRONGER THAN
NATURAL FAMILY RELATIONS

EXAMPLE: THE STORY OF ABRAHAM

Abraham wasn't accustomed to the idea of a God who gives. After all he had grown up as a worshiper of the moon, and the moon certainly never seemed interested in doing anything for Him.

Then he encountered El Shaddai, the greatest being of all—the one Almighty God. The first thing that this El Shaddai wanted to do was "give" to him. God's promises so astounded Abraham that he couldn't believe them. He asked, *Lord, how can I know I am really going to receive these things?* (Genesis 15:8)

God answered him by cutting a Blood Covenant with him. That covenant settled forever any question Abraham could ever have about God's love and loyalty. Once blood had been shed, he knew God meant what He said. In E.W. Kenyon's book, <u>The Blood Covenant,</u> he states, "We find that Abraham 'cut the covenant' with some of his neighbors before he ever entered into the covenant with Jehovah." He also states that he read a book by Dr. H. Clay Trumbull in which he showed there had been a Blood Covenant practiced by all primitive peoples from time immemorial. He proved that this Blood Covenant was the basis of all primitive religions. So when God said He wanted to cut covenant with Abraham, Abraham knew what that meant.

Abraham provides us with a model for responding to the living God. God loves you because you and He are connected by the pure covenant blood of Jesus.

God did the same for us! He cut a Blood Covenant with you and me, and He sacrificed His own son to do it. A Blood Covenant <u>demands,</u> <u>absolute,</u> <u>unwavering loyalty</u>. Jesus' broken body and shed Blood have become the eternal proof of God's love for you.

As author Max Lucado states: "The cross did what sacrificed lambs could not do. It erased our sins, not for a year, but for eternity."

Through Communion, God has urged you and me to remember the broken body and shed Blood again and again, so that when your faith in His promises begins to waiver, you might have a strong consolation. (Hebrews 6:18)

Also in E. W. Kenyon's book on <u>The Blood Covenant</u>. The silence of the disciples when Jesus introduced the Lord's Table, saying, *"This is My Blood of the New Covenant, which is poured out for many unto the remission of sins."*And then He told them to eat the bread, which was His body and to drink the wine which He declared was His Blood, I say, the very silence of the disciples indicates they understood what He meant. They already knew what was involved in making covenant. They were always asking Him questions about things they did not understand, but this they clearly understood.

Ask God to give you revelation knowledge about the Blood Covenant because it will strengthen your faith in God and in His promises.

We have a covenant with God, and this revelation will touch every aspect of your life.

> 1. It will help you receive your healing when you are sick.
>
> 2. It will give you confidence that God will meet your financial needs.
>
> 3. It will strengthen your marriage and family relationship.
>
> 4. It will bring peace to your mind, and joy to your soul.

FOUNDATION SCRIPTURES:

Genesis 12:1-8

Genesis 15:1-21

Genesis 17:1-11

Hebrews 6:13

Exodus 2:24-25

I.   THE POWER OF A BLOOD COVENANT

A. The Hebrew word "covenant" means "to cut, where or until the blood flows."

B. Stanley and Livingstone in Africa: the covenant was never broken.

C. God consulted Abraham (because he was in covenant with Him) before Sodom and Gomorrah were destroyed.

II. ALL BLOOD COVENANTS HAVE THREE BASIC REASONS FOR BEING CUT

A. Love and Devotion—Expression of dedication forever.

B. Protection—The stronger one becomes available to the weaker one.

C. Equality—One will not take advantage of the other.

III. THE POWER OF THE BLOOD COVENANT

A. The Covenant of Blood recorded by all ancient civilizations is the most powerful and serious form of agreement ever established. It is this form of agreement that God used to reveal His love to His people.

IV. TERMS OF THE BLOOD COVENANT

A. Families spent time together to determine the terms of the covenant.

B. The covenant was based on strengths and weaknesses, not on common traits.

C. Their strengths and weaknesses balanced each other out. A family that was weak in one area would bind themselves to another family that excelled in that particular area.

V. COVENANT SITE

A. A Covenant Representative was selected from each family.

B. At the covenant site, in full view of both families, an animal was killed. The animal was cut down the center (down the spine) and the halves were laid opposite each other, creating a walkway between them saturated with blood, called the "walkway of blood." (Genesis 15:9-10)

VI. COVENANT CEREMONY BEGINS

A. The covenant representatives remove and exchange coats as a symbol of the agreement between them.

The coat represented their tribe's identity, strength and authority. By exchanging coats, they symbolically exchanged authority. By giving each other their coats, they were saying, "All that I do, all that I am, and all that I have is now yours."

B. Next, they exchanged weapon belts containing their swords and shields, etc., saying "My strength is now your strength. Your enemies are now my enemies." They were saying they would fight one another's battles for them. Ephesians 6:10-17 talks about putting on the armor of God. This is a covenant statement.

VII. THE WALK OF BLOOD

A. Each representative paced twice through the blood-soaked path between the halves of the slain animal.

B. On each pass, they stopped, and standing in the midst of the blood, made promises to each other that could never be broken—the blessings of the covenant. They also stated the curse, or penalty, for breaking the promises.

C. They swore, with God as their witness that just as this animal had given its life, so they also would be willing to die to protect each other.

D. Then, the covenant representatives cut their hands and wrists so that blood would easily flow.

1. They bound their wrists together, allowing the blood to intermingle. This signified that the two were actually one, having the same blood. In more recent centuries, gun powder was used to make the scar more outstanding.

2. They swore by their God, raising hands so that both families could see the blood, and know that the covenant had been cut. God had now become a witness, and a third party to the covenant.

3. Then, the two families exchanged their names, and combined their names.

Example: When someone's last name has a hyphen between it, like Hammer-Smith. More than likely, covenant was cut between two families many years ago.

E. Finally, the covenant meal was shared. The elders of each family fed each other bread and wine saying, "This signifies my body and my blood. I'll die before I let anything happen to you. I am offering you my very life." They ate in remembrance the body (bread) and the wine (blood). Acts 2:42 refers to the covenant meal.

F. A relationship had been born. A bond had been made signifying covenant love and fidelity. In Hebrew it is called "Hesed;" in Greek it is called "Agape." It is a love that says, "I will never leave you nor forsake you." Jesus said, "It is My Blood which shall be shed for you." The disciples were familiar with covenant.

VIII. COVENANT EXAMPLES IN OLD TESTAMENT

A. God killed animals (shed blood) to prepare coats of skin for Adam and Eve. (Genesis 3:21)

B. In Genesis 22:16-18, Abraham received from God because he refused to let go of the covenant!

C. Moses received the Law (10 Commandments) and the priesthood. (Exodus 20:3-17)

D. David and Jonathan had a covenant relationship. (1 Samuel 18:1, 3-4)

IX. THE OLD COVENANT: THE BLESSING AND THE CURSE

A. The covenant between God and Abraham bound Abraham and his descendants to God, and God to them, with ties that could NOT be broken or dissolved!

B. The Blessing—Deuteronomy 28:1-14.

C. The Curse—Deuteronomy 28:15-61.

D. Jesus fulfilled this covenant in every way. His coming, His ministry, all of life, is the product of what God and Abraham agreed to. (Galatians 3:13-19)

E. Jesus became the curse, and destroyed its power. He gave Himself as the sacrifice—no more killing of animals—no more "temporary" atonement. The cross did what sacrificed lambs could not do—it erased our sins not for a year but for eternity!!

X. THE NEW COVENANT: A DECLARATION OF OUR LIBERTY

A. 1 Corinthians 11:24.

B. Matthew 26:27-28.

C. The New Testament—the copy of our Blood Covenant with God, as joint heirs with Jesus.

D. Jesus is the surety of the New Covenant. (Hebrews 7:22)

XI. THE BLOOD COVENANT: THE COVENANT OF STRONG FRIENDSHIP

A. Foundation Scriptures:

1. Ephesians 2:11-13.

2. James 2:23.

3. Isaiah 41:8-13.

B. Blood Covenant Friendship: The giving of one's total self in covenant faithfulness; in unreserved trust. We are knit together in Covenant Love. (Colossians 2:1-3)

XII. STRANGERS FROM THE COVENANTS OF PROMISE

A. What is "faith in Jesus' Blood"? (Romans 3:25)

B. What is the difference between Old Testament blood of animals that atoned for sin and the New Covenant

Blood of Jesus that reconciled and remitted? (Hebrews 9:8-14)

    1. Old Testament—for the flesh.

    2. New Testament—for the inner man.

C. Jesus was separated from the Father—not by His breaking of the Covenant, but by ours. (Hebrews 1:3-5)

D. He took away the First Covenant in order to establish the second one. (Hebrews 10:9)

    1. To open the way for us to enter into the holiest, and boldness as God's own children, priests and kings.

        a. Hebrews 6:19.

        b. Hebrews 10:14-22.

        c. Hebrews 9:12.

E. He established our covenant with God.

XIII. NO LONGER STRANGERS TO THE COVENANT OF PROMISE

A. Foundation Scriptures: Ephesians 2:12-19.

B. God is forever, irrevocably, covenant-bound to Abraham and his seed.

C. Unto thy seed have I given this land. (Genesis 15:1-18)

D. In their generations for an everlasting covenant, to be a God unto thee—and to thy seed after thee. (Genesis 17)

XIV. JONATHAN AND DAVID ENTER COVENANT

A. 1 Samuel 18:1-4.

B. When this covenant was made, it was the two of them, but God was present. (1 Samuel 18:3)

C. David is driven to give to Jonathan's seed for Jonathan's sake. (2 Samuel 9:1-11)

XV. JESUS—THE SEED ABOUT WHOM GOD WAS SPEAKING TO ABRAHAM

A. Galatians 3:15-16.

B. The Covenant promise raised Jesus the way David's promise raised Mephibosheth.

XVI. GOD IS FOREVER COVENANT BOUND TO ABRAHAM AND HIS SEED

A. Galatians 3:13-29.

B. Romans 4:16.

XVII. BE STRONG IN THE LORD AND THE POWER OF HIS MIGHT

A. Ephesians 6:10.

B. Take the weapons of God.

XVIII. KNOWLEDGE OF THE COVENANT GIVES STRENGTH TO THE INNER MAN

A. We lay hold to this hope. (Hebrews 6:13-20)

B. Strength in the inner man by the Holy Spirit. (Ephesians 3:14-21)

God and Jesus are in covenant together and we are joint heirs with Jesus once we accept Jesus into our hearts. We get to walk in all the blessings that the covenant provides.

In Genesis 17:7, God said to Abraham, *"And I will establish My covenant between Me and thee—to be a God unto thee, and to thy seed after thee."* God was promising to be their father and mother—the supreme provider of everything they would need in life. Deuteronomy 28:1-14 lists the blessings of God promised to those who will put His Word first place in their lives.

So to be pleasing to our Father, we need to receive all that He has provided for us! He is our Covenant Father and we are His Covenant children!

In Deuteronomy 28, we find the blessings promised to those who keep the terms of the agreement and also in that chapter we find the curses for anyone who breaks the agreement. This is where our covenant differs. Although we have been guilty of breaking the terms of the covenant, we have been set free from the penalty of it.

From the time Jesus was born until He died at Calvary, He never broke the terms of the covenant. <u>Yet when He went to the cross, He bore the curse for breaking it so that you and I would never have to bear it</u>. (Galatians 3:13-14)

He bore the penalty for your sin. He bore all your sicknesses and carried all your diseases.

He bore the curse for you and me so we could receive the blessings of Abraham through faith in Jesus Christ. (Galatians 3:29)

The Blood of Jesus has made the way for us to have a covenant relationship with our Father. Jesus became the sacrificial lamb that established your covenant with God. In Hebrews 10:19-22, the Word says we have a new and living way to approach God.

Jesus was not only the Blood sacrifice, but He also became our representative. (Remember when the tribes came together to make covenant, they each had a representative.) Jesus became that for us and is our mediator between God and man! We have an advocate with the Father, Jesus Christ the Righteous. (1 John 2:1) He forgives us when we confess our sins and He cleanses us from all unrighteousness. Jesus was the blood sacrifice and the representative, and He was also the covenant meal.

John 6:51 says, *I am the living bread which came down from heaven: if any man eat of this bread, he shall live forever: and the bread that I will give is My flesh, which I will give for the life of the world.*

As I said at the beginning of this chapter, as you hunger to know more about the Blood Covenant, you will see it more and more in the Scriptures. In Ephesians 6:10-11, 13-17—Jesus has exchanged His weapons and His armor with you and made you strong in the power of His might. He exchanged your weakness for His strength. Through this covenant relationship, you are now one with Him.

Since Jesus went to Calvary and shed His Blood for us, we have a New Covenant, a better covenant, and we do not have to receive any of the curses listed in Deuteronomy 28:16-68. We have been delivered from curses! This is part of our inheritance and we need to receive and walk in it and enjoy our freedom!

Jesus took your sin and gave you His robe of righteousness and right-standing with God. Just like the tribes in the covenant ceremony exchanged names and combined their names, God has given us the authority to use His name. We are His namesake! Mark 16:17 says, *and these signs shall follow them that believe; In My name shall they cast our devils.*

Remember, being in covenant means God wants to love you, protect you and provide for you! So walk in the fullness of all God has provided for you!

This is an example of how to pray for your protection by the power of the Blood of Jesus:

"Father, I thank You in the Name of Jesus, for the protection I have when I have faith in the power of the Blood. Right now I apply the Blood of Jesus to my home, the occupants, possessions, and I plead a Blood line over my property."

"Satan, I speak to you in Jesus' Name, and I proclaim that your principalities, powers, rulers of the darkness of this world and spiritual wickedness in heavenly places are bound from operating against me and my family in any way. I declare and decree we are all loosed from your assignment. We are all extremely healthy and prosperous because we are covenant children of our Covenant Father!"

NOTES

LESSON 7
PRAYER KEYS

INTRODUCTION

When you are going on a trip, you use a road map for directions. When we pray, we need direction to make certain that our prayers are lining up with the Word of God and leading us into the Throne Room of God. The five steps listed in this lesson will help you pray more effectively.

I.   IN THE NAME OF JESUS

A. Always pray to your Heavenly Father in the Name of Jesus. John 16:23-24, *And in that day ye shall ask me nothing. Verily, verily. I say unto you, Whatsoever ye shall ask the Father in my name He will give it you.*

B. v. 24, *Hitherto have ye asked nothing in My name: ask, and ye shall receive, that your joy may be full.*

C. In these verses, Jesus was telling His disciples that after He went to Calvary and had been raised from the dead, they were to pray to His Father. We see that our prayers should be made to our Heavenly Father in the Name of Jesus. According to Jesus' instructions, we are not to address our prayers to Him but to our Father.

D. We are under the New Covenant. We are under the protection of the Blood of Jesus that was shed at Calvary, so we are to pray to the Father in Jesus' Name.

E. When the disciples asked Jesus to teach them to pray, He taught them to say, *Our Father which art in heaven, Hallowed be Thy name....* (Matthew 6:9-13)

II.   THE WORD OF GOD

A. Base your prayers on the Word of God. For accurate prayers, pray God's Word back to Him. True prayer that touches God, is caused by the Word of God: John

15:7-8, *if ye abide in Me, and My words abide in you, ye shall ask what ye will and it shall be done unto you.*

v. 8, *Herein is My Father glorified that ye bear much fruit: so shall ye be My disciples.*

1. Whatever your situation is, go to the Word of God for your answer. Find your promise and stand on it. Don't back down once you have found a promise in the Word of God. Be aware of the tactics of the devil. He wants to come to steal the seed of the Word of God's promise from you. He will try to instill unbelief in you and make you think God's Word will not work for you. *The thief cometh not but for to steal, and to kill, and to destroy; I am come that they might have life, and that they might have it more abundantly.* (John 10:10) Jesus wants you to live free from the devil's tactics.

2. When you go to the Word of God for your promise, you build your prayer life on a strong foundation: *Heaven and earth shall pass away, but My words shall not pass away.* (Matthew 24:35) *Call unto Me, and I will answer thee, and shew thee great and mighty things, which thou knowest not.* (Jeremiah 33:3) What wonderful scriptures! What wonderful promises from the Word of God.

B. It is important that we:

1. Praise and worship God—come before Him with a humble and thankful heart.

2. Pray for revelation of the Blood Covenant so we can know what is rightfully ours because we are God's covenant children and He is our Covenant Father. He wants nothing but the best for us. Know that we can come boldly into His Throne Room.

3. Read and study the Word of God. (Proverbs 4:20-23)

4. Find His promises in His Word that cover your situation and be fully persuaded that His Word <u>will</u> come to pass! Say "I lay claim to what is mine!"

5. Thank God for the answer to your prayers <u>before</u> you see the answer.

III. FORGIVE WHEN YOU PRAY

A. Be sure that unforgiveness is not found in your heart:

Mark 11:25-26, *And when ye stand praying, forgive, if ye have ought against any: that your Father also which is in heaven may forgive you your trespasses.*

v. 26, *But if ye do not forgive, neither will your Father which is in heaven forgive your trespasses.*

Colossians 3:13, *Forbearing one another and forgiving one another, if any man have a quarrel against any, even as Christ forgave you, so also do ye.*

B. When you were born again, you received grace, God's grace. The same grace you received will help you forgive others.

1. When you realize that someone has hurt you or cheated you and hard feelings toward that person keep coming to the surface, repent and forgive quickly. It is a scheme of the devil to keep you from walking in love and to keep you from having your prayers answered.

2. Recognize immediately where unforgiveness is coming from and get rid of it. It opens the door for Satan to come into an area of your life, and it will keep you from having your prayers answered: *For we wrestle not against flesh and blood, but against principalities, against powers, against the rulers of the darkness of this world, against spiritual wickedness in high places.* (Ephesians 6:12) Jesus said in Matthew 5:44-45, *...Love your enemies, bless them that curse you, do good to them that hate you, and pray for them which despitefully use you and persecute you.*

v. 45, *That ye may be the children of your Father which is in heaven.*

C. If we want to be a blessing to God, we will do what His Word says to do, rather than what the world's system dictates. We will pray for God's mercy to be poured out on those who persecute us. When we do what His Word says, we are pleasing our Heavenly Father.

   1. When you forgive others, you will have peace of mind. When you hold on to unforgiveness you carry around "excess weight." But what peace of mind you'll find when you leave it at the feet of Jesus, never to pick it up again. You will experience spiritual victory.

   2. You will recognize your own spiritual maturity made evident by the joy you are experiencing. You will find it easier to forgive because you have purposed in your heart not to be offended. Because you have not allowed that stronghold to be a part of your life, Satan is being defeated.

IV. BELIEVE YOU RECEIVE WHEN YOU PRAY AND BE SPECIFIC

A. *Therefore I say unto you, What things so ever ye desire, when ye pray, believe that you receive them, and ye shall have them.* (Mark 11:24)

B. Years ago, when my son was in his third year of college, I sold our home and moved into an apartment. It did not take me long to find that I would rather have a home than an apartment. So, when he graduated from college, we both agreed to look for another home. Immediately following our decision, the rent on our apartment was raised so we quickly began "taking steps." We sat down and prayed the prayer of agreement on the specifics we desired for another home. Because God had already done so many miracles in our lives, we knew nothing was too hard for Him. Our specifics were:

Specific #1—That the rent would be less than $200.00 per month!

Specific #2—That the house would be available before the end of the month.

Specific #3—That the house would have a view of the water (the town we lived in was surrounded by water, and this was something we had wanted for years).

Specific #4—That the house would have a fireplace. In less than two weeks' time we found a house (the second one we looked at) with all of the four "specifics" we had (in advance) prayed, believed and thanked God for!

C. God was once again showing His grace, mercy, and faithfulness. He wants to bless His children when they come to Him in complete confidence and trust. Praise His holy Name! *Delight thyself also in the Lord: and He shall give thee the desires of thine heart.* (Psalm 37:4, Matthew 21:22)

D. Smith Wigglesworth said: "There is something about believing God that will cause Him to pass over a million people to get to you."

V. LET THE HOLY SPIRIT PRAY THROUGH YOU

A. Romans 8:26-27, *Likewise the Spirit also helpeth our infirmities: for we know not what we should pray for as we ought: but the Spirit itself maketh intercession for us with groanings which cannot be uttered*

v. 27, *And He that searcheth the hearts knoweth what is the mind of the Spirit. Because He maketh intercession for the saints according to the will of God.*

This passage of Scripture should help answer any questions you might have about praying in tongues (i.e., "Is it really for today?").

1. The Word of God is true. I know the difference in my prayer life before I received my heavenly language and after I began praying in tongues. There was such a release in my spirit when

the Holy Spirit began to flow through me. It's a beautiful experience—no wonder the devil tries to deceive people into thinking it is not for today. We experience victory through the power of the Holy Spirit.

B. When we allow the Holy Spirit to pray through us, or allow Him to help us, we will see answers to our prayers. Paul said the Holy Spirit would help us in our prayer life: *...for we know not what we should pray for as we ought: but the Spirit itself maketh intercession for us.*

VI. WAITING FOR PRAYERS TO BE ANSWERED

NOTE: Some of our prayers are answered immediately, some within a week or a month, and others take a while. But, every time you bow your knees, lift your head and your hands toward heaven, calling out to God in faith, He hears you! Your prayers will be answered in His timing, not in ours!

A. Examples of Waiting for Prayers to be Answered

1. Anna and Simeon: a lifetime. (Luke 2:25, 36-38)

2. Daniel: twenty-one days. (Daniel 10:13)

3. Moses: eighty years. (Hebrews 11)

4. Abraham: a lifetime. (Hebrews 11)

5. Noah: one hundred twenty years. (Genesis 6:3)

6. Caleb-Joshua: forty years. (Numbers 13:14)

7. Jeremiah: seventy years. (Jeremiah 18)

8. Elijah: three and one-half years. (1 Kings 18)

9. David: youth/manhood (1 Samuel 16:13)—he went eight to thirteen years after being anointed before he walked in the office of King.

10. Joseph: three years. (Genesis 39)

NOTES

LESSON 8
BECOMING AWARE OF HIS PRESENCE

INTRODUCTION

You must be willing to pay the price to get where you want to be, or where you need to be, in your day-to-day relationship with God. Do you want to be a success in life? Of course you do! Then be willing to develop a quality prayer time. The key to a successful prayer time is found in the word commitment.

This chapter is made up of three parts:

Part One—Preparation for Developing a Quality Prayer Time

Part Two—Praise: the Highest Form of Intercession

Part Three—Worship: a Form of Prayer

Be determined to be established and grounded in the Word of God. Be determined to praise and worship God every day. By the leading of the Holy Spirit, a prayer life will be birthed in you through commitment and through the things you will learn in this most-important chapter.

PART ONE

PREPARATION FOR DEVELOPING
A QUALITY PRAYER TIME

INTRODUCTION

"We hear much in this day of the superiority of outward expressions of worship and a devotion concentrated in specific acts at fixed times. But unless there are such fixed acts, there will be little diffused devotion—if there are no reservoirs, there will be no water in the pipes—if a man does not pray at definite times, and that daily, he may talk as he likes about all life being worship, but 'anytime' will soon come to mean 'no time'." (Alexander MacLaren, 1826-1910)

NOTE: John 4:24 tells us that *God is a Spirit: and they that worship Him must worship Him in spirit and in truth*. We know that we can pray to God and worship Him anywhere and at any time. However, this lesson is primarily for those who are just beginning to develop a prayer life and for those who have been unable to discipline themselves to have a specific prayer time.

I.   A SPECIAL PLACE

The special place we choose for our daily prayer time should be:

A. A place where we are comfortable;

B. A place where we will not be interrupted; and

C. A place where we can be with God and daily know the joy of His presence.

II.   A SPECIFIC TIME

A. We need to be committed to a specific prayer time. We need to make our prayer time top priority in our lives.

B. We must not break our daily appointment with God.

C. If we will be disciplined in our time with God, He will honor our prayer time.

III. A PURPOSE

The purpose of a prayer time is to develop closeness with God.

IV. STARTING POINT

When you first start your time of prayer, begin small! Start with five to ten minutes each morning (or whatever time it is you are praying). When you are comfortable with that amount of time, move on immediately by increasing your time to fifteen or twenty minutes. NEVER let yourself "rest" where you are. Discipline yourself: tell your flesh what to do; don't let your flesh dominate you!

A. Discipline—don't live your life aimlessly. Discipline directs the power so it is channeled properly. The amount of discipline you allow in your life determines how fast you go and how far!

B. Discipline yourself to be a winner for God! Every day of our life should be dedicated to fulfilling the call God has placed on our lives! Make yourself a vessel yielded to the Holy Spirit so that He may flow through you.

C. Make plans to place yourself in the presence of God every day or to become aware of His presence every day. Your heart will stay soft in His presence!

V. A SPIRIT OF EXPECTANCY

A. We should go to meet God daily with a spirit of expectancy. There is nothing "dull" about our Heavenly Father, His Son, Jesus, and the Holy Spirit. We are the ones who make things "dull" or uninteresting.

B. Procrastination: We increase our own stress level when we procrastinate.

C. Always make a record. Take a notebook. God will share things with you in your prayer time. Sometimes He will remind us of a letter we need to write or a call we need to make. Sometimes He will give us revelation knowledge of a particular scripture in the Bible. Sometimes He may give you inspiration for a song or a book that He wants you to write or ideas for a new business.

1. God will show you how to spend your money or how to invest it wisely, etc.

D. Thanksgiving: When thanksgiving is in our heart, it is easy to pray. It is the clutter and "busyness" of life that makes prayer difficult. Get into an attitude of thankfulness, and prayer will come easy to you.

E. Prayers are living memorials before God! (Acts 10:4) We have a standing invitation to come boldly into the throne of grace that (you) may obtain mercy, and find grace to help in time of need. (Hebrews 4:16) "Obtain" means "to get possession of."

VI. DO NOT ACCEPT A SPIRIT OF GUILT

A. After we make a quality decision—a commitment to God—to have a specific prayer time, our lives will run more smoothly, and we will be at peace with God and with ourselves. But be prepared, for the devil will try to come at you from every angle. Remember, he is a defeated foe!

1. James 4:7 says, *Submit yourselves therefore to God. Resist the devil, and he will flee from you.* Jesus fought the devil with the Word of God and kept saying, "It is written. Get thee hence, Satan." (Matthew 4:4, 7, 10) Don't ever let Satan discourage you from praying!

B. Sometimes we may miss our prayer time with God. We feel guilty because several days have passed since our last prayer time. Then the devil begins to accuse us: "You are no good anyway. You will never be able to have a daily prayer time. God is not pleased with you."

A spirit of guilt will try to put you in bondage. This spirit of condemnation is from the devil, not God.

C. We all struggle with our prayer time (e.g., it is easy to miss prayer time while we are staying at someone else's home; we try to conform as much as possible to their schedule rather than to ours). Whenever (and for whatever reason) we miss our prayer time, we need to keep trying and ask the Holy Spirit to help us remain diligent and faithful to our commitment.

D. God has great plans for you! Instead of running *from* God, run *to* Him. He knows the whole situation any way! Go to Him, repent and receive His forgiveness, then start your prayer time all over again. God loves you; He knows your heart, and He is just waiting for you to come back and talk with Him.

VII. PREPARE YOUR HEART

A. We need to prepare our hearts before we start praying.

We can do this by:

1. Have a heart "check-up." Be sure we're walking in love and forgiveness.

VIII. GOD'S PRESENCE

A. Have you ever noticed that you become like the people you are around the most? When you spend time with God, you will start thinking like He thinks—and talking like He talks—His image will begin to shine forth in you.

B. The greatest joy we can ever receive is to be in the presence of God, and this is possible at all times because the Holy Spirit abides in us.

C. Joy is not found in traveling, sports, TV, shopping, getting a bigger house, new cars, or buying more property. (All of these things are fine in their proper place, but we must not make them "idols." We must keep God first.) "Things" are only temporary and will only bring temporary joy because we can see, feel, and touch them. But the things of God, which are unseen, are eternal. (2 Corinthians 4:18)

D. Daily coming into God's presence or becoming aware of His presence, blesses Him as much as it does us. We receive peace and joy in His presence. (In Parts Two and Three we will see how praise and worship helps train and develop our spirit man to become aware of the presence and direction of the Holy Spirit.)

IX. RECEIVING A PRAYER LIFE

A. In John 15:7, Jesus said: *If ye abide in Me, and My words abide in you, ye shall ask what ye will, and it shall be done unto you.* This is the key—this is the answer—the Word abiding in us will bring forth a prayer life! The Word of God will stir your spirit to seek God.

1. Worship God, pray in the Spirit, and read the Word. When your heart is full of the Word of God, then you're ready to get on your knees and seek Him! God honors His Word: you will be praying His Word back to Him.

2. When you are abiding in His Word—when you are full of His Word—the Holy Spirit will fill you with a desire to praise God, a desire to worship Him and to linger in His presence every day.

3. When you abide in His Word, a prayer life will be born!

NOTE: Again I want to say there is no set way to pray! It pleases God for us to just desire to be in His presence. The Holy Spirit will direct you.

NOTES

PART TWO

PRAISE: THE HIGHEST FORM OF INTERCESSION

INTRODUCTION

In Part One, we learned of one way to develop a quality prayer time. Now we are ready to enter God's presence with praise and worship. In this lesson we will discuss praise, because praise "opens the door" for worship.

All prayer should begin with praise. When we truly learn to praise God and to come before Him with a grateful and thankful spirit—really delighting to be in His presence—we will find that nothing else really matters.

I. PRAISE GOD IN ALL SITUATIONS

Praise will set us free from bondage. When we praise God, we recognize and make known the greatness of what He has done.

   A. "Praise" means the act of glorifying or extolling God (Webster's Third New International Dictionary).

   B. Praising God in all situations is completely foreign to man's intellect or reasoning. However, the Word of God commands us to praise God in all situations.

   1. Philippians 4:4-7, *Rejoice in the Lord always: and again I say, Rejoice*. This means to have joy. We don't see many people who have joy today.

   v. 5, *Let your moderation be known unto all men. The Lord is at hand.*

   v. 6, *Be careful for nothing: but in everything by prayer and supplication with thanksgiving let your requests be made known unto God.*

   v. 7, *And the peace of God, which passeth all understanding shall keep your hearts and minds through Christ Jesus.*

   2. Romans 8:28, *And we know that all things work together for good to them that love God, to them*

who are called according to His purpose. This promise is to those who love God and are called to God's purposes.

3. Psalm 37:4, *Delight thyself also in the Lord; and He shall give thee the desires of thine heart.*

   a. When God is our delight, He will see to it that we have the desires of our heart. When He is top priority in our life, the desires of our heart will be in line with His will.

   b. Just knowing that we are in God's perfect will can give us peace!

4. Nehemiah 8:10, *...for the joy of the Lord is your strength.*

II. PRAISE: AN ACT OF THE WILL

A. Praising (or delighting in) God is simply an act of the will. When we release ourselves to praise God—as we raise our hands in surrender to His care, placing every situation and every circumstance at His feet—we show Him that we have complete trust and confidence in Him.

B. Praising God is not a result of feelings. Sometimes we just do not "feel" like praising or worshipping God. However, it does not matter how we feel, we should command our flesh to obey our spirit.

   1. Our spirit constantly wants to praise and worship God because it responds directly to the wishes of the Holy Spirit. If we respond to the Holy Spirit and refuse to let our flesh dominate us, our lives will be completely changed for the glory of God!

III. PRAISE: A WEAPON OF OUR WARFARE

A. Praise is one of the weapons God has given us that will defeat the devil. Therefore, it needs to be a major part of our personal prayer time and of our church services.

1. Praise not only lets God know that we love Him and that He is top priority in our lives, but it also informs the devil that we know God is omnipotent: He is our God!

B. We need to sing the Word of God! When we enter into praise with the power of the Word of God, we tear down strongholds of the devil. The longest book of the Bible (Psalms) is a book of music!

   1. "Tehilim" is a musical term and is the Hebrew word for psalm.

   2. "Psalmoi" is the Greek word for psalm. It means "sacred songs sung to musical accompaniment."

   3. If we feel discouraged or oppressed, we should lift up our hands and sing praises to God. We can sing our way into victory!

   4. *And at midnight Paul and Silas prayed and sang praises unto God and the prisoners heard them.* (Acts 16:25) Paul and Silas may have been in prison, but they had learned how to receive victory! They did not complain to God about the problem; they worshiped Him for the solution!

C. Praise and worship are weapons of our warfare and will pull down strongholds. (2 Corinthians 10:3-5; Ephesians 6:12)

   1. Praise will set us free from bondage. God's power is released in praise and worship and brings us healing and deliverance: *Now the Lord is that Spirit: and where the Spirit of the Lord is, there is liberty.* (2 Corinthians 3:17)

IV. **PRAISE, PLANS AND PURPOSES**

A. God has a purpose for our lives, and He has placed this purpose within our spirits. Therefore, we should always have our thoughts turned toward God so that we can hear what He is saying to our spirit.

B. When we are praising God and truly delighting in Him, the Holy Spirit can reveal to us God's plans and purposes for our lives.

    1. When He reveals His plans to us, we are not to moan, groan, complain or say "I will never be able to do that!" Instead, we need to rejoice (Philippians 4:4-7); the Holy Spirit will give us the ability to do all that God tells us to do!

    2. What He reveals to us to do is always bigger (in the natural) than anything we could possibly ever do. He wants us to depend on Him. He will make divine and glorious connections, and help us get the job done!!!

V.   PREPARING TO PRAISE

A. Be honest with God—He knows your heart anyway! He is not looking for silver or gold vessels but for "yielded" ones. We need to have every part of our being yielded to Him.

NOTE: One of the biggest stumbling blocks in the Body of Christ is that many Christians have accepted Jesus as their Savior but have never surrendered every area of their life to Him as Lord. They hold back the areas they still want to control. I heard someone say, "Any area of your life that you try to 'justify' is the area of your life that you are not willing to give up." When this occurs, they are usually holding onto man-made doctrines instead of the Word of God. We need to realize that the Word of God will set us free to praise and worship God as He created us. Once we have decided to live by the Word of God, we will not care what people think of us; totally ingrained in our spirit will be the truth that the Blood of Jesus that was shed at Calvary has redeemed us from sin, sickness, disease, and poverty! We should be excited about praising God every day for the rest of our lives because of all that was provided for us at Calvary! We will then begin to live

77

lives of victory and not of defeat! That is something to praise God for and to shout about!

B. If we do not feel comfortable praising God (perhaps because of our previous religious training), we should just tell God! Once we accept Jesus as Lord and Savior, the Holy Spirit resides inside of us to lead and guide us. He is the Spirit of Truth. We can ask the Holy Spirit to be our Helper and to teach us how to praise God.

C. Examples of Praise

1. Sometimes as I kneel before God, I quote Psalm 51:10: *Create in me a clean heart, 0 God; and renew a right spirit within me.* Then I pray along these lines.

    "Father, I come to You now in the name of Jesus. I come by way of Calvary, by the Blood of Jesus, and I ask You to forgive me for anything I have said or done, or for any thoughts that were not pure. Only You, Father, know that I want the motives of my heart to be pure so that You can use me.

    I love You, I worship You, and I adore You. You are the only Father I have ever known, and knowing You and loving You has made my life complete. Though I truly want to walk in love toward everyone, I sometimes blow it. So, Father, please forgive me. Holy Spirit, I ask You to correct me so there will be no unforgiveness in my heart.

    Father, the desire of my heart is to be a yielded vessel for the Holy Spirit to flow through to help carry out Your plans and purposes on the earth. Holy Spirit, I ask for a fresh infilling of You, I want to be led and controlled by You. I ask You to search me and point out the things I may not be aware of so I might repent quickly.

    Holy Spirit, I thank You for teaching me how to praise and worship God more, and how to worship and glorify Jesus.

2. Some people might say that I do not need to do all of that before I start worshipping God, but I want to be honest before Him and get rid of any "garbage" that may have collected. (This does not mean that I am right and someone else is wrong. This is just the way I enter in.) I talk with God all day long because I enjoy His fellowship. However, the best part of my day is the morning. This is my "special time" of praise, worship, praying in the Spirit, and reading God's Word. I hunger and thirst for more of God each day. My goal in life is to be a blessing to Him every day. But you know, the more I pray, the more I worship; the more I read God's Word, the more I know I have only just begun—I realize how little I really know.

3. The sooner we start praising God all day long, and having a thankful heart, the more blessings are going to come into our lives.

VI. THANKSGIVING: A STEPPING STONE INTO PRAISE

A. We are now ready to come into God's presence with thanksgiving. We need to thank Him and praise Him for all that He has done for us.

1. Thank and praise Him:

   a. For His Holy Name (call out His names, Lesson 9, and what they mean);

   b. For His presence that abides in us;

   c. For His Son, Jesus;

   d. For His plan of Salvation (that we have been redeemed from the curse of sin, sickness, disease and poverty, weariness, and discouragement);

   e. For His Holy Spirit;

   f. For His Holy Word;

g. For the Blood of Jesus that protects us, redeems us, cleanses us, heals us and reconciles us, gives us boldness, and gives us overcoming power;

h. For our church and pastor;

i. For the roof over our head, clean water, clean linens; and

j. For family and friends.

2. The more we praise and thank God, the more we will become aware of His presence. God's Word says that He inhabits the praises of His people: *But thou art holy, O thou that inhabitest the praises of Israel.* (Psalm 22:3)

VII. CONCLUSION

A. Deuteronomy 28:47-48 warns of what can happen when we do not praise God. You will become slaves to your enemies because of your failure to praise God for all that He has given you.

1. We should praise God continually.

2. Habakkuk 3:17-18, *Although the fig tree shall not blossom, neither shall fruit be in the vines; the labour of the olive shall fail, and the fields shall yield no meat; the flock shall be cut off from the fold, and there shall be no herd in the stalls.*

v. 18, *Yet I will rejoice in the Lord, I will joy in the God of my salvation.*

NOTES

PART THREE

WORSHIP: A FORM OF PRAYER

INTRODUCTION

Our number one goal in life should be to please God! We need to declare this every day. Praising and worshipping God can become as normal as breathing, He is our Abba Father. He is our Covenant Father, and we are His Covenant Children. He longs to fellowship with us; He created us to fellowship with Him.

I. THE MEANING AND PURPOSE OF WORSHIP

A. In Part Two, we talked about praising God. Thanksgiving and praise opens the door for us to go into the Holy of Holies and worship our Heavenly Father.

1. Worship must honor God. The Hebrew word for worship is "chavah," meaning to bow down or to prostrate oneself before anyone to do him honor and reverence.

2. Worship is a form of prayer—it means to humble oneself and to submit, as in Psalm 95:6, *O come, let us worship and bow down: let us kneel before the Lord our Maker.*

3. The English word "worship" comes from the Old English word "weordhscipe." It was later shortened to "worthship." In English law it is still used when the judge is referred to as "your worship." The word worship also means to adore, esteem, magnify, revere, venerate, exalt.

B. It is hard for us to understand worship without relating it to a movement of the body. In Leviticus 9:24, the people fell face down before the Lord. They fell under the power of God. Sometimes we bend our knees, sometimes we stretch out our hands, and sometimes we do both.

C. In the New Testament, the word used most for worship is "proskuneo." It is a combination of two separate Greek words: "pros," which means towards, and "kueneo," which means to kiss: so "proskuneo" means to kiss towards. In Luke 7:37-38 we have an example of this type of worship:

v. 37, *And, behold, a woman in the city, which was a sinner, when she knew that Jesus sat at meat in the Pharisee's house, brought an alabaster box of ointment.*

v. 38, *And stood at His feet behind him weeping, and began to wash His feet with tears, and did wipe them with the hairs of her head and kissed His feet, and anointed them with the ointment.*

1. What a beautiful example of worship. This woman was aware that the people who were gathered around Jesus knew she was a sinner, but she did not care. She just wanted to come and bring the best that she had—the precious ointment—and wanted to worship at Jesus' feet in complete abandonment to "self." This is the place that God wants us to come: to love, worship, and adore him more than anyone or anything else!

2. Man was created to worship God.

D. We find in Matthew 4:9-10 how Satan tried to tempt Jesus in the wilderness and what Jesus' reply was to his temptation: *...All these things will I give thee, if Thou will fall down and worship me. Jesus replied, Get thee hence Satan: for it is written, Thou shalt worship the Lord thy God, and Him only shall thou serve.*

II. CREATED TO WORSHIP

A. Right here would be a good place to stop and examine ourselves as to the direction of our worship. We must remember that we will ultimately end up serving whatever it is we worship. We were created to worship, and we should be worshipping God. But if we are not, then we are probably worshipping money, cars, big houses, sports, TV, more property, our husbands, our wives, our children, our grandchildren, food, etc. Whatever we worship we will end up serving!

B. When Jesus, in John 4:21-24, was speaking to the woman at the well, He was telling her that spiritual worship is required:

v. 21, *Jesus saith unto her, Woman, believe Me, the hour cometh, when ye shall neither in this mountain, nor yet at Jerusalem, worship the Father.*

v. 22, *Ye worship ye know not what: we know what we worship: for salvation is of the Jews.*

v. 23, *But the hour cometh, and now is, when the true worshippers shall worship the Father in spirit and in truth: for the Father seeketh such to worship Him.*

v. 24, *God is a Spirit and they that worship Him must worship Him in spirit and in truth.*

C. In these four verses of scripture, Jesus used the word "worship" eight times. In John 8:28 and 38, Jesus tells us that He speaks only what the Father tells Him to speak. The Bible is our book of instruction, and God says we must learn to worship Him in spirit and in truth. When we worship in spirit and in truth, that is a love relationship. (John 4:24)

1. "In spirit" means in supernatural strength and power: *Not by might nor by power, but by My spirit, saith the Lord of hosts.* (Zechariah 4:6) "In truth" means "in reality". The Greek word for "in" means "in oneness with."

D. Matthew 13:44 says, *Again, the kingdom of heaven is like unto treasure hid in a field: the which when a man hath found he hideth, and for joy thereof goeth and selleth all that he hath, and buyeth that field.* This is the way we should feel about wanting more of God— to have a spiritual hunger to get to know Him better every day. We should all want to invest in that kind of treasure—not what we can see, feel, and touch (because those things are temporary)—but to see the things of the Spirit (which are eternal), where our Heavenly Father, Jesus, and the Holy Spirit are. We need to pray that we will invest in the Kingdom of Heaven, for that is where our citizenship lies when we are born again.

E. God is looking for worshippers. Worshippers will come to a place of freedom, victory, and liberty because worship will bring you into God's presence.

III. WE ARE THE TEMPLE OF THE HOLY GHOST

A. Our bodies are the temple of the Holy Spirit, and the purpose of a temple is to be used for worship: 1 Corinthians 6:19-20, *What? Know ye not that your body is the temple of the Holy Ghost which is in you, which ye have of God, and ye are not your own?*

v. 20, *For ye are bought with a price: therefore glorify God in your body, and in your spirit, which are God's.*

B. We need the Holy Spirit to help us worship God: *For we are the circumcision, which worship God in the spirit, and rejoice in Christ Jesus, and have no confidence in the flesh.* (Philippians 3:3) Worship is a love relationship between you and God.

C. Our Heavenly Father is searching for people who will do what they have been created to do: WORSHIP HIM. He loves you so much, He sent His only Son to die for your sins (John 3:16), and He wants you to make Him top priority in your life—to love Him and show your love by worshipping Him. Worship is a love relationship between you and God.

CONCLUSION:

In the presence of the Lord is fullness of joy, and when you are full of the joy of the Lord, then you have the strength to do whatever He wants you to do.

There is no set formula on how to worship, just be honest and real with God. Surrender to Him, and let the Holy Spirit teach you. Get on your knees every day, stretch your hands toward heaven, and tell Him how much you love Him—that is a good place to begin!

NOTES

LESSON 9
NAMES OF GOD

INTRODUCTION

We need to study the names of God and what they mean. The names of God relate to His character and tell us who He is. God is not in heaven just so we can call on Him for help. He created you and me to worship Him, to praise Him, and to glorify His name. We need to be able to call out His names and what they mean as we come before Him in praise and worship.

In John 17:6, 26, Jesus prays His high-priestly prayer and says, *I have manifested Thy name unto the men which Thou gavest Me out of the world....*

v. 26, *And I have declared unto them Thy name, and will declare it: that the love wherewith Thou hast loved Me may be in them, and I in them.*

The most important of all the names that God was called in the Old Testament was Jehovah—the Covenant Name of the God of Israel. It denotes the "unchangeable one," the eternal "I AM." (Exodus 6:3, Psalms 83:18, Isaiah 12:2; 26:4)

At first, only the consonants which formed this name were written YHVH or JHVH. Then, the vowels had to be supplied by the reader. His name was regarded so sacred that in reading, it was customary to not pronounce it out loud, but to substitute Adonai or Lord. The original pronunciation was probably "Yahveh" or Jahveh." This name was revealed to Moses in Exodus 6:3. To Moses, it was the Covenant Name by which God was known to His Covenant People.

NAME	MEANING
Elohim	My Creator, His Greatness and Glory—creative and governing power—God of might and strength. (Genesis 1:1-2; 2:4; 3:2, Exodus 9:30)
Yahweh or **Jehovah**	Comes from the Hebrew word "to be"—He who causes everything to be. He possesses essential life, permanent existence. (Exodus 3:13-15) Jehovah means "the Lord is God," the one to be worshiped—divine majesty and power.
El Shaddai	Hebrew word for "breast"—the one who nourishes us and satisfies us with an abundant supply. The All-Sufficient One. (Genesis 49:24-25)
Adonai	Adon or Adonai "Lord, Master"—speaks of ownership—indicates that God is owner of each member of the human family and that He demands our complete obedience to Him. (Psalm 110:1)
Jehovah-Jireh	"God will provide." He sees our needs and provides for them. (Genesis 22:14, Romans 8:32, Philippians 4:19)
Jehovah-Rophe	*"I am the God that healeth thee."* (Exodus 15:26, Isaiah 53:5, 1 Peter 2:24) He heals us spiritually, physically, and mentally. *He forgives all thine iniquities, and heals all your diseases.* (Psalm 103:3)
Jehovah-Nissi	"The Lord my banner," Jesus is our banner; He is our Victory! (Exodus 17:15, Romans 8:31, 37, 1 Corinthians 15:57, 2 Timothy 1:10, Hebrews 2:14-15)

NAME	MEANING
Jehovah-M'Kaddesh	"Jehovah who sanctifies" (sanctify means to dedicate, to consecrate, or make holy, or to set apart). Holiness is an attribute of God. It is the nature of God to make His people holy. (1 Corinthians 6:11, Hebrews 13:12)
Jehovah-Shalom	"Jehovah is Peace." Jesus is called the Prince of Peace. There is peace that takes place between God and man because of atonement. Being justified by faith, we have peace with God. (Judges 6:23-24)
Jehovah-Tsidkenu	"Jehovah our Righteousness." His righteousness is given to us by the Blood of Jesus as a free gift through faith. (Romans 5:17-19, 2 Corinthians 5:21)
Jehovah-Rohi	"Jehovah my Shepherd." God leads us, provides for us, feeds us, and protects us. He is the good Shepherd. (Psalm 23, John 10:27-28)
Jehovah-Shammah	"Jehovah is There." Our sins are forgiven, and we can receive the fullness of the Holy Spirit. The Holy Spirit is always present. We are the temple of the Holy Spirit. (Ezekiel 48:35, 1 Corinthians 3:16, Revelation 21:3)

NOTES

LESSON 10
PUTTING ON
THE FULL ARMOR OF GOD

INTRODUCTION

Jesus has already won the victory for us at Calvary. We need to keep ourselves prepared to walk in that victory by putting on the full armor of God every day. When we put on this armor we are obeying the Word of God, and this builds a hedge of protection around us. Christians must wake up and be aware of what is going on in the world!

I. WHAT THE ARMOR IS

A. Paul tells us to put on the armor of light and commands, *But put ye on the Lord Jesus Christ.* (Romans 13:12, 14)

B. In Ephesians 6:10, "power" is the Greek word "kratos" and means "ruling power." "Might" is the Greek word "ischus" meaning "endowed power." Ruling power here refers to STABILITY IN LIFE. Paul is saying— be STABILIZED, having the inner power which keeps you always upright. Ruling power is on the inside of your spirit. The eternal life of God is inside of you. STABILITY is a godly key to excellence, and to excellence of ministry. That ruling power was endowed to you the moment you accepted Jesus Christ as your Savior.

Jesus wants to be our defense and to clothe us with Himself. (Ephesians 6:10-18)

v. 10, *Finally, my brethren, be strong in the Lord, and in the power of His might* [ruling power, endowed power].

v. 11, [You] *Put on the whole armour of God, that ye may be able to stand against the wiles of the devil.*

["Standing" means to hold your ground. Once you have taken the high ground, hold on to it. Plant your flag and don't budge against the wiles—tactics or strategy—of the devil].

v. 12, *For we wrestle not against flesh and blood, but against principalities, against powers, against the rulers of the darkness of this world, against spiritual wickedness in high places.*

v. 13, *Wherefore take unto you the whole armour of God, that ye may be able to withstand in the evil day, and having done all to stand.*

v. 14, *Stand therefore, having your loins* [the loins represent the emotions—we are not to let our emotions rule us] *girt about with truth, and having on the breastplate of righteousness* [a part of the inner man].

v. 15, *And your feet shod with the preparation of the gospel of peace.*

v. 16, *Above all, taking the shield of faith, wherewith ye shall be able to quench all the fiery darts of the wicked.* [The Blood of Jesus ministers defeat to unclean spirits.]

v. 17, *And take the helmet of salvation, and the sword of the Spirit, which is the word of God:* [Jesus' name means salvation and salvation means deliverance, healing, soundness of mind, and security.]

v. 18, *Praying always with all prayer and supplication in the Spirit, and watching thereunto with all perseverance and supplication for all saints.*

II.   APPLYING THE ARMOR OF GOD

A. The following chart shows how we should apply the armor of God each day:

APPLYING THE ARMOR OF GOD		
Armor	Declaration	God's Promises
I gird my loins with the belt of Truth.	Jesus You are my Truth.	*I am the way, the truth, and the life...* John 14:6
I strap on the breastplate of Righteousness.	Jesus, You are my Righteousness.	*For He hath made Him to be sin for us, Who knew no sin: that we might be made the Righteousness of God in Him.* 2 Corinthians 5:21
I shod my feet with preparation of the gospel of peace. These are my "go ye" shoes to go ye into all the world to spread the gospel.	Jesus, You are my preparation, my readiness.	*I can do all things through Christ which strengtheneth me.* Philippians 4:13
I hold up the shield of Faith so I am able to quench all the fiery darts of the wicked.	Jesus, You are my faith. I refuse to be hurt or offended.	*So then faith cometh by hearing, and hearing by the word of God.* Romans 10:17

I place the Helmet of Salvation on my head	Jesus, You are my Salvation. Jesus, your Name means salvation and salvation means deliverance, healing, soundness of mind and security. I receive what You have already provided for me and I thank You for it.	*Much more then, being justified by His blood, we shall be saved from wrath through Him. For if, when we were reconciled to God by the death of His son, much more, being reconciled, we shall be saved by His life.* Romans 5:9-10
I hold up the Sword of the Spirit, which is the Word of God.	Jesus I declare that You are my living word.	*No weapon that is formed against thee shall prosper and every tongue that shall rise against thee in judgment thou shalt condemn. This is the heritage of the servants of the Lord, and their righteousness is of Me, saith the Lord.* Isaiah 54:17

B. Paul tells us in Ephesians 6:10-12 that in order for us to be strong we must put on the whole armor of God that we might be able to stand against the deceits of the devil. He warns us that we are not fighting against flesh and blood, but against powers and rulers and spiritual wickedness in high places.

C. In the hour we are living in, daily putting on the full armor of God is as important as putting on our regular clothes.

1. We must be obedient to God's Word. He has given us the Bible as our book of instructions, so that we might walk in victory. In this passage in Ephesians, He outlines for us what we must do to overcome the tactics of the devil.

2. Paul reminds us, and we must remind ourselves, that it is not a battle in the natural, but a battle in the spirit. Jesus has already won the battle for us, now it is up to us to walk in the victory!

III. PUTTING ON THE ARMOR OF LIGHT

A. We began this lesson by quoting Romans 13:12, 14, *But put ye on the Lord Jesus Christ.* Also in Romans 13:12, it says, *The night is far spent, the day is at hand: let us therefore cast off the works of darkness and let us put on the armour of light.* In John 12:46, we read that Jesus says, *"I am come a light into the world, that whosoever believeth on Me should not abide in darkness."*

B. We see that Jesus is the light of the world, and when we put on the Lord Jesus Christ, who is the light of the world, we are putting on the armor of light.

1. The armor of light dispels the darkness.

2. Wherever we are and wherever we go, when we take time daily (before we ever go out the door) to put on the full armor of God, the enemy has to flee! We must be obedient to the Word of God!

NOTES

LESSON 11
WHAT IS PRAYER?

INTRODUCTION

Prayer is that special something that satisfies the cry, or void, within every human being. People without a life of prayer will try to satisfy that cry (or that "longing" or "void") with alcohol, drugs, fancy cars, fast cars, sex, shopping, etc. These "things" can never satisfy man's "inner being" because they are not of God. Only the things of God can give glory to Him and bring inner peace that man and the world are so desperately seeking.

Prayer is the key to the heart of God! The Bible teaches from cover to cover that God's connection with man is a prayer and faith connection. When you see Him act in a mighty way, you may be sure that there was someone, somewhere, praying, and interceding to bring Him on the scene.

The Word of God tells us that *God is a Spirit: and they that worship Him, must worship Him in Spirit and in truth.* (John 4:24) Jesus says in Luke 18:1, *...men ought always to pray and not to faint.* We were created to fellowship with God. Only a life of prayer can bring true happiness.

Praise is the highest type of prayer. When you spend time with God, praising and worshipping Him, and finding out His will, it will keep you from being a selfish, self-centered person. You forget about "us four and no more!" God will show you a nation to pray for, or you'll go to buy something for yourself, and you'll buy two of them, and give one away. God does not bless stingy or lazy people!

I. WHAT IS PRAYER?

A. Prayer is:

1. Answering the call in the Word of God. *Call unto Me, and I will answer thee, and shew thee great and mighty things which thou knowest not.* (Jeremiah 33:3)

2. The lifeline from your knees to the Throne Room of God.

3. Trusting God and not man.

4. Visiting and talking with God.

5. Experiencing God's presence every day.

6. Fellowshipping with God the Father.

7. Prayer is carrying out God's will upon the earth.

8. Prayer is joining forces with God our Father.

9. Bringing the power of God into your life so strongly that it causes you to love even the worst of your enemies.

10. The highest form of communication—communication between our covenant Father and His covenant children.

    a. When God sent His only Son, Jesus, to the cross of Calvary, and that middle wall or partition (veil) was torn down, a call was sent forth from the Father to His children to come and commune with Him.

11. A binding force. John Wesley said, "Prayer binds Satan and releases God!"

12. The development of spiritual sensitivity within an individual.

13. An avenue to God's glory. As you continue in prayer, God's glory is released.

14. Unselfish; true prayer forgets "self" and prays for all men without ceasing.

15. Having a need in your life, and calling out to God by faith in the Name of His Son, Jesus. You will have a feeling of calm assurance in your heart when you know that God has heard you—that all has been taken care of in the Throne Room of your God. (Philippians 4:4-8, 1 Peter 5:7)

16. Revelation on the Word of God. *Open Thou mine eyes, that I may behold wondrous things out of Thy law.* (Psalm 119:18)

17. Bringing the supernatural into the "natural." Andrew Murray said, "Prayer can do anything God can do."

18. God's saints cooperating with Him in bringing His plans and purposes for their lives from heaven to earth.

II. CONCLUSION

Elijah was a man of prayer! God supplied for him supernaturally. (1 Kings 17:1-7)

God is our total source of supply, and when we have a prayer life, God is obligated to meet our needs!

NOTES

LESSON 12
WHY A LIFE OF PRAYER?

INTRODUCTION

God will take a "nobody" and make them into a "somebody" in His kingdom when they are dedicated and committed to a life of prayer. All souls won on the streets were first won in prayer. Every convert is the result of the Holy Spirit's leading in answer to the prayers of some believer.

I.   WHY A LIFE OF PRAYER?

A. Jesus is our role model, and He led a life of prayer.

  1. Sometimes Jesus rose up before daybreak to pray; at other times He prayed all night. In Mark 1:35 we read, *And in the morning, rising up a great while before day, He went out, and departed into a solitary place, and there prayed.*

B. In Matthew 14:14-25, we see where Jesus fed the five thousand and then sent the disciples out in the boat while He separated Himself on the mountain to pray. In verses 23-25 we read:

  v. 23, *And when He had sent the multitudes away, He went up into a mountain apart to pray: and when the evening was come, <u>He was there alone</u>.*

  v. 24, *But the ship was now in the midst of the sea, tossed with waves: for the wind was contrary.*

  v. 25, *And in the fourth watch* [which is between 3:00 A.M. and 6:00 A.M.] *of the night Jesus went unto them, walking on the sea.*

  1. We see that Jesus' life was a life of prayer, dedicated to carrying out His Father's will. His life of prayer was an example for the disciples to see and to follow. How can you carry out the Father's will if

you haven't been talking to Him to find out what His will is?

2. We are His disciples on the earth today, and we need to commit ourselves to a life of prayer. When we do this, God's anointing will fall on us when we stand up to teach, preach, lay hands on the sick, or cast out demons in Jesus' name!

    a. You might say, "But Jesus was the Son of God." That is true, but He came on earth as a man. He had a job to do for His Father. He needed to be in communication with His Father to get His instructions. And so it is with you and me—we need to be in communication with our Father, daily getting instructions to fulfill the call on our lives, being sure that the flesh is not getting in the way, but that we are being led by the Spirit of God, the Holy Spirit.

D. Job 21:15 says, *What is the Almighty, that we should serve Him? And what profit should we have, if we pray unto Him?* Sound familiar? These are two questions the wicked (or the unsaved people) will ask you and me. (It's amazing, but they were asking the same questions in Job's day!):

1. "Why should I serve God? I am getting along fairly well by myself, doing just what I want to do." (In other words, serving their flesh); and

2. "Hey, what's in it for me? What will I get out of all this?"

E. God Almighty compares those who do not pray with the wicked: *Pour out Thy fury upon the heathen that know Thee not, and upon the families that call not on Thy name.* (Jeremiah 10:25) God says those who do not pray are like the heathen, or the wicked.

1. In Isaiah 52:1, people who are prayerless are compared to people who are spiritually asleep, and cannot see the move of the Holy Spirit.

2. If you are prayerless, the power of God cannot come on your life.

3. When we don't pray, we actually sin against God! *Moreover as for me, God forbid that I should sin against the Lord in ceasing to pray for you: but I will teach you the good and the right way.* (1 Samuel 12:23)

4. The devil will try to keep you from developing a prayer time but we've been given power and authority over the devil.

F. Jesus prayed His High-Priestly prayer to His Father, asking that we might be one as He and His Father are one. (John 17:21)

1. When we pray for unity in the Lord Jesus, then we can come together in one accord.

2. The power that is in prayers prayed in one accord can change nations and can bring harmony into our government, our churches, and our families, and can keep our own lives in harmony with God's perfect will.

NOTES

LESSON 13
WHAT PRAYER WILL DO
FOR YOU

INTRODUCTION

We may set many goals for our lives and take on many projects, but without prayer it will all come to naught!

I. A LIFE OF PRAYER

A. Prayer is the key to a fulfilling relationship with God that brings you an inner peace and excitement—every day is a new venture with God.

1. The inner peace that is developed through a life of prayer is something no one can take from you.

2. When you keep the peace that God gives you (Jehovah-Shalom), you know that no matter what situation arises that day, God will be right there beside you!

B. Kathryn Kuhlman said, "Prayer keeps you refreshed."

1. Prayer will keep your thoughts pure; it will help you keep a clean mind.

2. When you are committed to a life of prayer, God will not waste your talents and your abilities. The Holy Spirit will give you the ability to do whatever God is calling you to do.

C. When you have a life of prayer, you will be in the perfect will of God.

1. When you are quiet before God, the Holy Spirit will reveal directions to you for your life.

2. Having a life of prayer does not mean that situations and circumstances will not surface in your life, but it does mean that you will meet every situation with spiritual maturity.

3. There is a "built in" quietness, assurance, and confidence in knowing that you are not facing a problem alone—that God is with you and that He is bigger than any problem you will ever have.

D. As you yield to a life of prayer and you are "abiding" in His Word, God will put His desires in your heart: *Delight thyself also in the Lord; and He shall give thee the desires of thine heart.* (Psalm 37:4)

1. *He is the vine, and we are the branches.* (John 15:1-8) As you grow in the Lord, you will be able to trust the desires of your heart.

2. Remember this, God never calls us to a task without giving us the equipment to fulfill the task.

E. When you develop a strong prayer life, your character becomes stable.

1. Have you ever noticed that people who do not take time to pray are inconsistent in their character? They stay confused.

2. We must get to know the Holy Ghost. He will help you get rid of wrong motives. Wrong motives will cause you to yield to a spirit of manipulation just so that you may get your own way.

F. When you have developed a prayer life, you forgive, walk in love, and have your wounds healed quickly.

1. If we would be honest, we would admit that we are all hurt by others from time to time. One great benefit of a life of prayer is that we realize the source of the hurt. We realize that the devil is trying to get us discouraged and trying to get us to open a door to unforgiveness by being easily offended.

2. Your prayer life, your close walk with God, will cause you to be an overcomer in every situation!

II. THE POWER OF PRAYER

A. God moves through the power of prayer to direct the darts of the evil one away from His prayer warriors, placing His saints in a position of victory.

   1. God is a God of victory, and He wants us to walk in victory!

   2. Elijah prayed and a child came back to life.

   3. Hezekiah prayed and lived fifteen years longer.

B. S. D. Gordon said, "If a man be right and put the practice of praying in the right place, then his speaking, serving, and giving will be fairly fragrant with the presence of God." He also said, "The greatest thing that anyone can do for God and man is to pray. Prayer is the winning blow." E. M. Bounds said, "God shapes the world by prayer. The more prayer there is in the world, the better the world will be, the mightier the forces against evil."

C. Prayer will bring strength into your life. Matthew 9:22 says, *Daughter be of good comfort, thy faith hath made thee whole.*

III. PRAYER IS HELPING GOD

A. *And He saw that there was no man, and wondered that there was no intercessor: therefore His arm brought salvation unto him; and His righteousness, it sustained him.* (Isaiah 59:16) God needed someone to intercede.

B. *And I looked, and there was none to help; and I wondered that there was none to uphold: therefore Mine own arm brought salvation unto Me; and My fury, it upheld Me.* (Isaiah 63:5)

C. *And I sought for a man among them, that should make up the hedge, and stand in the gap before Me for the land, that I should not destroy it but I found none.* (Ezekiel 22:30) God needed someone to stand in the gap.

D. Prayer makes us wait on God and avoid serious mistakes. It clears up our vision by opening our spiritual eyes.

E. Prayer activates our faith and replaces anxiety with peace.

IV. HOW TO HANDLE GRIEF

A. However painful our moments of grief, we are not to play mind-games with questions about faith! Instead, we seek the Author of our faith. God did not design our pain. He is not indifferent to what is happening. We must learn to "rest" in Him. Job 5:8-9 says, *As for me, I would seek God, and to God I would commit my cause—who does great things and unsearchable, marvelous things without number.*

B. We must go to the very heart of God. Matthew 11:28 says, *Come unto me all you who are weary and heavy laden, and I will give you rest.*

1. The ultimate center of life is "In Him." Don't be disappointed, or even surprised, when life deals a blow that forces you to retreat to the Savior.

2. Even when our understanding ends, and our disciplines fail, the Savior is still there. Seek Jesus. He satisfies—after all and above all.

NOTES

LESSON 14
HINDRANCES TO PRAYER

INTRODUCTION

Whatever hindrances are in your life to keep your prayers from being answered—you need to take authority over the devil. In Matthew 28:18, the Greek word translated "power" is also translated "authority." So, Jesus was saying, "All power (authority) is given unto me both in heaven and in earth." Jesus took His authority and delegated it to believers—to the church.

Matthew 28:19-20, *Go ye therefore, and teach all nations, baptizing them in the name of the Father, and of the Son, and of the Holy Ghost.*

v. 20, *Teaching them to observe all things whatsoever I have commanded you: and, lo, I am with you always, even unto the end of the world. Amen.*

Mark 16:15-17, Jesus is actually saying, "In My Name believers shall exercise authority over devils." Put the devil on the run with the Word of God. God's Word stands behind the authority He has given us.

Do something about the adverse circumstances in your life by taking authority over Satan and stand your ground against him with the Word, claiming what belongs to us.

Each believer has to take authority over the devil for himself. James 4:7 says, *"Submit yourself to God; resist the devil and he will flee from you!"*

In 1 Peter 5:8-9, the devil is not trying to devour sinners—they already belong to him. He's seeking to devour Christians.

Ephesians 4:27 tells us*, neither give place to the devil.* Don't give place by having the wrong attitude.

1. Don't re-think past annoyances.

2. Repent quickly.

3. Push your wheelbarrow upside down!

Ye did run well; who did hinder you that ye should not obey the truth? (Galatians 5:7)

I.   REVIEW

We are going into the fourteenth chapter on prayer. It is now time to have a "check-up" on our prayer life.

   A. We know (or are learning):

      1. The importance of being saved and born again;

      2. The importance of being filled with the fullness of the Holy Spirit;

      3. "Who" the Holy Spirit is;

      4. God's covenant with man and our rights because of the Blood shed at Calvary;

      5. The Blood Covenant;

      6. Prayer keys, to teach us how to pray;

         a. That we need a special, quiet place for our prayer time, and a selected time to pray;

         b. That we need to enter into His gates with thanksgiving and into His courts with praise, (That if we want to learn more about praise and worship, the Holy Spirit will teach us "how" if we ask Him.);

         c. The names of God and what they mean.

         d. How to put on the full armor of God; and

         e. What prayer is: that we must pray God's Word back to Him; that we must believe we receive when we pray; that we must be honest with God; that we must be led by the Holy Spirit; and, that we must be specific when we pray.

   B. But yet we know deep down (in our spirit man) that something is not right. These questions keep coming to our minds:

      1. Am I praying correctly?

2. Does God really hear my prayers?

3. If God does hear my prayers, why is it taking so long for an answer?

C. Remedy: Each day we need to ask the Holy Spirit to search us out and to point out those areas in our lives where we have fallen short so that we might repent: *Create in me a clean heart, O God; and renew a right spirit within me.* (Psalm 51:10)

1. We need once and for all to cast down all doubt, unbelief, and fear.

II. PRIDE: A MAJOR HINDRANCE TO PRAYER

A. A major hindrance to answered prayer is pride.

1. Pride was the downfall of Satan.

2. Pride will stand up and say, "I am going to live MY life the way I want to. No one is going to tell me how to live my life." That kind of pride is really saying: "I can do it better than God!"

B. Pride always leads to the sins of rebellion and unfor-giveness.

1. When we make a choice to do things our own way, we come into conflict with God's plan for our life.

2. When we are born again, we daily need to denounce pride in our lives and ask the Holy Spirit to help us develop a teachable spirit. *...God resisteth the proud, but giveth grace unto the humble.* (James 4:6)

3. Rebellion is of the devil, and the Bible says it is equal to witchcraft: *For rebellion is as the sin of witchcraft, and stubbornness is as iniquity and idolatry. Because thou hast rejected the Word of the Lord, He hath also rejected thee from being king.* (1 Samuel 15:23)

a. EXAMPLE: When runaway teenagers at Daytona Beach, Florida, were interviewed, each said if they could do it over again they would stay home. They had rebelled against their parents and had not heeded their advice. Some said that even though their parents were not always what they should have been, life at home was better than selling their bodies on the street (like they were having to do now just to survive).

III. LACK OF COMMITMENT TO PRAYER LEAVES AN OPEN DOOR FOR PRIDE AND REBELLION

A. In 1 Samuel 15:23 we see that God did not want to appoint a king over Israel. However, the people kept coming to Samuel and demanding that they have a king.

1. God told Samuel that Saul (a young man out looking for his father's strayed donkeys) would be coming that way. God told Samuel to anoint Saul as king. God even gave Saul a new heart: *And it was so that when he had turned his back to go from Samuel, God gave him another heart: and all those signs came to pass that day.* (1 Samuel 10:9)

2. Saul was the first king of Israel. He could have been a great king, but he wanted to "do his own thing"—he wanted to have things his way. He never developed a life of prayer. He depended on Samuel to do all of his praying because Saul knew Samuel heard from God.

   NOTE: How many times do we listen to that old sin nature calling us to come back into that from which we have been delivered? We fall away by listening to the voice of our so called "friends" rather than to the voice of God.

3. 1 Samuel 15:24-26 says:

   v. 24, *And Saul said unto Samuel, I have sinned: for I have transgressed the commandment of the*

114

Lord, and thy words: because I feared the people, and obeyed their voice.

v. 25, *Now therefore, I pray thee, pardon my sin, and turn again with me, that I may worship the Lord.*

v. 26, *And Samuel said unto Saul, I will not return with thee: for thou hast rejected the word of the Lord, and the Lord hath rejected thee from being king over Israel.*

B. Because Saul lived a life that was not dedicated to prayer, pride crept in. Notice that in verse 24, Saul says that he feared the people and obeyed their voice. That is what we do today when we choose to listen to what the world says is the popular thing to do.

1. If you have developed a strong prayer life, you will immediately recognize the difference between the voice of God and the voice of the devil.

2. Because of prayerlessness, a spirit of rebellion against God entered Saul's life. Because of prayerlessness, Saul lost his kingdom. Think about this and weigh the results of the choices you have to make each day.

IV. OTHER HINDRANCES TO PRAYER

A. Walking in unforgiveness—holding on to a grudge.

1. A husband's prayers may not be answered if there is unforgiveness toward his wife. *Likewise, ye husbands, dwell with them according to knowledge, giving honour unto the wife, as unto the weaker vessel, and as being heirs together of the grace of life; that your prayers be not hindered.* (1 Peter 3:7)

B. Thoughts of unworthiness—thinking you are not good enough and that you must get your life cleaned up before your prayer life can begin, Jesus will accept you right where you are once you are born again by the Spirit of God.

Thoughts of unworthiness will leave you completely when you have the *eyes of your understanding enlightened.*

Ephesians 2:1-2, 4-6 tells us what our position in Christ is:

1. Joint seating with Christ Jesus, the Anointed One, is *"far above all principalities and powers of darkness."* Evil spirits can't influence the believer who has joint-seating with Christ far above all principalities and powers.

2. Our seating and reigning with Christ in heavenly places is a position of authority, honor, and triumph—not failure, depression, and defeat.

3. As a believer, your seating with Christ is part of your inheritance NOW!

4. We need to exercise our rightful authority!

C. Thoughts of hopelessness—thinking that it is too late in your life for you to change. The devil will tell you that you will never be any different—that you were born the way you are, and there is nothing you can do to change. That is a lie from the devil. The resurrected power of the Lord Jesus Christ is more powerful than any lie from Satan.

1. The power of the Blood of Jesus that was shed at Calvary will help you be an overcomer! Revelation 12:11 tells us: *And they overcame him by the Blood of the Lamb and by the word of their testimony: and they loved not their lives unto the death.*

D. Doubt and unbelief.

1. You have been told that the Bible is a book of instruction for you—that you can find promises in God's Word. Stand on God's Word and believe that His promises will come to pass. It all seems too good to be true, yet it is true!

2. You must believe God's Word is written for you. Find scriptures that apply to your situation and

meditate on them day and night: *But his delight is in the law of the Lord; and in his law doth he meditate day and night.* (Psalm 1:2) *And this is the confidence that we have in Him, that, if we ask any thing according to His will, He heareth us.*

v. 15, *And if we know that He hear us, whatsoever we ask, we know that we have the petitions that we desired of Him.* (1 John 5:14-15)

E. Sin.

Psalm 66:18 says, *If I regard iniquity in my heart, the Lord will not hear me.* Isaiah 59:1-2, *Behold the Lord's hand is not shortened, that it cannot save; neither His ear heavy, that it cannot hear.*

v. 2, *But your iniquities have separated between you and your God, and your sins have hid His face from you, that He will not hear.*

F. Not considering the poor. We need to keep our hearts tender toward the needs of God's people: *Whoso stoppeth his ears at the cry of the poor, he also shall cry himself, but shall not be heard.* (Proverbs 21:13)

G. Having idols in your life. God must be the top priority in our lives: *Son of Man, these men have set up their idols in their heart, and put the stumbling block of their iniquity before their face: should I be inquired of at all by them?* (Ezekiel 14:3)

H. Praying selfish prayers. *Ye ask, and receive not, because ye ask amiss, that ye may consume it upon your lusts.* (James 4:3)

I. MAJOR HINDRANCES TO PRAYER

A. Listed below are major hindrances that will keep you from developing a life of prayer:

Anger	Gossip	Self-Pity
Competition	Haughtiness	Strife
Critical Spirit	Jealousy	Unbelief
Depression	Judgmentalness	Unforgiveness
Doubt	Unteachableness	Envy
Rebellion	Wrong Attitudes	Fear
Selfishness	Self Centeredness	Pride

B. Many people think they are the only ones with these "hang-ups." But you need to know that lying spirits straight from the devil are trying to convince you that you are all alone in your "hang-up."

1. Christians should not be in bondage. YOU CAN BE SET FREE. The Word of God says, *and where the Spirit of the Lord is, there is liberty.* (2 Corinthians 3:17)

2. We are to be free to fellowship with God and to have the prayer life we desire.

NOTES

LESSON 15
PRAYER AND FASTING

INTRODUCTION

Fasting is a discipline that needs to be developed in a Christian's life as much as the discipline for prayer. Prayer and fasting go hand in hand. If you have things in your life for which you have been diligently seeking an answer from God, you may need to set aside time for prayer and fasting.

Always consult a doctor before fasting. Fasting helps to clean out your body. It is a healthy thing to do.

Fasting is a way of humbling yourself. But, fasting for the sake of fasting is useless. It must be at the direction of God. Isaiah 58 describes the fasting approved by God. The key to a right relationship with God is obedience. Procrastination will put you in bondage. We need to read about the promises that will come forth from God as we are obedient to His call to fast! (See also Matthew 17: 20-21.) *Pg 1439*

I. PRAYER AND FASTING IS SCRIPTURAL

A. There are two kinds of fasting: personal (or individual) and collective. In collective fasting, a group of individuals agree upon a purpose for their fast and upon the desired results for which they are believing to receive from God. *Pg 1297 Read All Footnote*

   1. In Joel 1:14, we read, *Sanctify ye a fast, call a solemn assembly, gather the elders and all the inhabitants of the land into the house of the Lord your God, and cry unto the Lord.*

   2. Christians need to realize the importance of fasting and prayer in connection with the outpouring of God's Spirit.

B. Moses, Elijah, and Jesus are three Biblical characters who fasted forty days.

121

1. *And when He had fasted forty days and forty nights, He was afterward an hungered.* (Matthew 4:2)

    Pg. 1416

2. In Matthew 6:1-18, Jesus gives instructions to His disciples on three duties: <u>giving alms</u>, <u>praying</u>, and <u>fasting.</u> He warns them to check out the motives of their hearts.

    Pg 1528

3. We read in Luke 4:1-2 that immediately after Jesus was baptized in the River Jordan by John the Baptist, He was led by the Holy Spirit to spend forty days fasting in the wilderness.

4. You are not being encouraged to fast forty days! I am just pointing out that fasting is scriptural. Fasting is not intended to make you, or those around you, miserable! God will give you the grace to develop this discipline in your life.

C. Others in the Bible who prayed and fasted:

    Jonah 3:5-10. Pg 1328 repented because of Judgements

    Nehemiah 1:4-11. Pg 719 prayer of Intercession for a people

    Daniel 9:3-4. Pg 1267 prayer for Sin: Rebellion against God.

    Daniel 9:21-23.

    Daniel 10:2-3. Fasted and prayed for victory over Satan's power.

D. Acts 13:1-3.

    v. 1, *Now there were in the church that was at Antioch certain prophets and teachers, as Barnabus, and Simeon that was called Niger, and Lucius of Cyrene, and Manaen, which had been brought up with Herod the tetrarch, and Saul.*

    v. 2, *As they ministered to the Lord, and fasted, the Holy Spirit said, Separate me Barnabus and Saul for the work whereunto I have called them.*

    v. 3, *And when they had fasted and prayed and laid their hands on them, they sent them away.*

    1. As we, a body of believers, yield to coming into the unity that Jesus prayed we would (John 17:21-22)

and yield to the power that is released in prayer and fasting, sin will be driven out of the camp and the glory of God will be manifested in our midst!

II.   REASONS WHY WE FAST

A. The following are some of the reasons for fasting:

1. Fasting helps you have dominion over your flesh. You bring your body into subjection. (Galatians 5:17)

2. Fasting helps you be more sensitive to the leading of the Holy Spirit so that you can be led to do God's will and not your own.

3. When our motives are pure, prayer and fasting can break the bands of evil and help the oppressed go free. (Jesus gave an example of this in Matthew 17:18-21.)

4. Fasting was practiced by Jesus Himself. (Luke 4:1 -2) He fasted before entering into His public ministry.

5. Fasting is a way of humbling yourself.

6. Prayer and fasting are sources of strength and deliverance. Through prayer and fasting, we release God's power in our lives. Done correctly, fasting will bring deliverance and victory into our lives. (2 Chronicles 20:1-30, Ezra 8:21-23)

    NOTE: These are scriptures of victory as a result of collective fasting and praying.

III. SUGGESTIONS FOR INDIVIDUAL FASTING

A. Decide the purpose of your fast. Write down the things you are praying and fasting for, and put a date by them. Later you can go back and read this and you will be encouraged to be as disciplined about your days of fasting as you are about your times of prayer.

B. Prayer and fasting are scriptural, so enter your fast with positive faith. When we enter a fast with the right motive, our prayers will be answered. In Matthew 6:18, Jesus gave us this promise: ...*Thy Father, which seeth in secret, shall reward thee openly.*

C. If you are just beginning the discipline of fasting, start off by fasting one or two meals. Gradually build up to a day or two. Do not come under a spirit of condemnation if you fail the first few times you try. Just be determined that this is a discipline that will be developed in your life. Ask the Holy Spirit to help you resist the temptation for food.

    1. Some people drink only water during a fast, some drink fruit juices. Ask the Holy Spirit to direct you as you fast.

    2. When you are coming off your fast, let it be a gradual process. Use fruit juices, jello, and broths—things that are easily digested.

D. An absolute must during a fast is to feed your spirit with the Word of God! Read your Bible out loud and pray. Psalms is a good book to read. The Word of God ministers to your spirit and gives you supernatural strength.

NOTES

LESSON 16
PRAYERS IN ACTION

INTRODUCTION

It is not possible to cover every prayer need in this one chapter. I wanted to give you examples of praying God's Word. You and I, as individuals, are responsible for developing our own prayers. The Holy Spirit is the greatest teacher. God's Word is His will so we know when we pray the Word of God and pray in the spirit, we have offered up accurate prayers. Just use whatever part of these prayers the Holy Spirit directs you to use.

PRAYER FOR AMERICA AND THOSE IN AUTHORITY

Father, we come to You in the Name of Jesus, and we thank You for America. We pray that we will not take our freedom for granted, but will thank You for our country every day and declare that Jesus is Lord of America! We thank You for Your promise in 2 Chronicles 7:14 which says, *If My people, which are called by My name, shall humble themselves, and pray, and seek My face, and turn from their wicked ways; then will I hear from heaven, and will forgive their sin, and will heal their land.* We pray for a spirit of prayer to cover our land, for we see in 2 Corinthians 3:17 that it says, *Now the Lord is that Spirit and where the Spirit of the Lord is, there is liberty.*

We thank you, Father, that in Your Word it says, *Blessed is the nation whose God is the Lord....*(Psalm 33:12) We thank You for that blessing, and we declare that You and You alone are our High Tower. (Psalm 18:2) Father, we thank You that America was established on prayer, and we pray that we will be drawn back to our spiritual heritage. We declare that America will not continue to hurt because of prayerlessness! We are believing for a mighty outpouring of Your Spirit in our land, and we pray that it will begin within each one of us!

Search us, Holy Spirit of God, and point out those areas that are not pleasing in God's sight. Help us to daily repent according to Your Word in 1 Corinthians 11:31-32 which says, *For if we would judge ourselves, we should not be judged. But when we are judged we are chastened of the Lord, that we should not be condemned with the world. We pray, Father, that You create in us a clean heart. 0 God; and renew a right spirit within us.* (Psalm 51:10) Father, let that be the cry of our hearts so that we might be used by You to carry out Your plans and purposes in the earth today: *For the eyes of the Lord run to and fro throughout the whole earth, to shew Himself strong in the behalf of them whose heart is perfect towards Him.* (2 Chronicles 16:9)

Father, we pray for spiritual revival in America that would cause us to be aware of the holiness of God, and that we might be aware of the need to win lost souls to You. We know that true revival brings the presence and the conviction of the Holy Spirit. We believe that absolutely nothing can take the place of Your people coming before You in unity of the Lord Jesus, bowing their knees and seeking Your face.

We thank You that Your Word is true and will not return unto You void. We thank You that in Isaiah 55:11 You say, *So shall My word be that goeth forth out of My mouth: it shall not return unto Me void, but it shall accomplish that which I please, and it shall prosper in the thing whereto I sent it.* So, according to Your Word in 1 Timothy 2:1-2, *we pray for all men and women in authority...that we may lead a quiet and peaceable life in all godliness and honesty.*

We pray for our President of these United States, that he will be a man of prayer. We pray, Father, that he will see the wisdom of starting out each day on his knees, calling out to You for Your direction, wisdom, and discernment to be imparted to him in every decision he has to make. Thank You, too, Father, for raising up mighty prayer warriors to stand in the gap for our President and his family day and night. May we always have a president who loves America and seeks to defend her traditional values and the great legacy of freedom handed down to us.

We pray for our Vice-President, for the President's Cabinet, our Senators, Congressmen, House of Representatives, the Supreme Court Judges, the Governors of each state, the Mayors of every town and city, the Sheriffs' Departments and our Policemen. We declare by faith that they are godly people and that they will not listen to the counsel of the ungodly, according to Psalm 1:1, *Blessed is the man that walketh not in the counsel of the ungodly, nor standeth in the way of sinners, nor sitteth in the seat of the scornful.* We pray the Word of God over these people in authority and say, *And wisdom and knowledge shall be the stability of thy times, and strength of salvation: the fear of the Lord is His treasure.* (Isaiah 33:6) Lord, we pray that You grant our leaders wisdom, encouragement, and vision. Keep them from entering temptation and let their family relationships be strengthened.

Thank You, Father, that the righteous will be exalted and the wicked put down, and that our leaders see the wisdom and necessity for restoring prayer back into our schools. It is in Jesus' Name we pray. AMEN.

PRAYER FOR PASTORS, EVANGELISTS & TEACHERS

Father, we come to You now in the Name of Jesus, and we pray for godly pastors, evangelists, and teachers. We thank You, Father, that we can pray Your Word over Your servants (or Your sons and daughters). We see in Joshua 1:8 that as they meditate in Your word day and night they shall be prosperous and have good success. We thank You that they will not listen to the counsel of the ungodly according to Psalm 1:1, *Blessed is the man that walketh not in the counsel of the ungodly, nor standeth in the way of sinners, nor sitteth in the seat of the scornful but they hear and know the voice of the Good Shepherd, and they follow His voice and His voice only.* (John 10:27) We declare that the words that come out of their mouths will be words of faith, love, and power, because God honors words that line up with His Word. We declare that these, Your servants, will give no place to the devil (Ephesians 4:27) by letting words of fear, doubt, or unbelief come out of their mouth. Luke 12:29 tells us not to be of a doubtful mind: *For God hath not given us the spirit of fear: but of power, and of love and of a sound mind.* (2 Timothy 1:7)

We thank You for Psalm 91, and we pray this Psalm over every Godly pastor, evangelist, and teacher. We declare that they will dwell in the secret place of the most High and trust in You and You alone, Father, to be their refuge and fortress; that they will go forth each day confidently assured that no evil will befall them nor any plague come near their dwelling, for You have given Your angels charge over them to keep them in all their ways. Because they have chosen to abide in You, they can call on You in time of trouble and You will deliver them and honor them.

I pray, Father, that each pastor, evangelist, and teacher will start out each day seeking Your face, on their knees with their hands lifted up, worshipping and praising You for who You are and for Your mercy and grace. I thank You that they will call unto You for Your wisdom (according to Proverbs 4:5-9 and James 1:5-8) to be imparted to them in every decision that must be made that day—that they will be yielded to Your precious Holy Spirit to flow through them, to lead them, to guide them (John 16:7, Amplified), and to give them spiritual discernment. I thank You, Father, that as they yield to the leading of the Holy Spirit, they will realize that supernatural strength is flowing through them and equipping them for the task that must be done.

Father, we pray that they will realize they cannot answer the High Call of God on their lives in their own strength, but as they lean on and trust in You (Proverbs 3:5-6) they will be amazed at how much more You are able to accomplish through them in a shorter period of time. I thank You, Father, that their minds will be garrisoned with Your peace according to Philippians 4:7, and that they will go forth into each day filled with Your joy, not weighted down with burdens. (Philippians 4:4, John 17:13)

We thank You for the expectancy that is being developed in their inner being because they have started off the day in Your presence, worshipping and praising You. They have received assurance for the day that Your promises are true and that Your Word will not return unto You void. (Isaiah 55:11)

Thank You, Father, that their lives will line up with the Word of God: God first, family second, and ministry third. We thank You that the members of their families will become mighty prayer warriors, and that the members of their staff will be faithful and loyal—people who lead lives committed to prayer unto You.

What a comfort, Father, to know that we can stand on Your promises in Your Word and pray Isaiah 54:17 over these godly servants: *No weapon that is formed against thee shall prosper and every tongue that shall rise against thee in judgment thou shalt condemn. This is the heritage of the servants of the Lord, and their righteousness is of Me, saith the Lord.* We thank You, Father, for encouraging them today and for keeping them from entering into temptation. Let their family relationships be strengthened.

We pray this prayer in the Name of Jesus, and we give You all glory, honor and praise! AMEN.

PRAYER FOR STUDENTS

Father, we come to You in the Name of Jesus, and we pray a hedge of protection around every student. (Psalm 91:9-11) We pray that each day they will ask for a fresh infilling of the Holy Spirit to lead them and guide them. We pray that they will daily seek Your presence and worship and praise You, asking for Your wisdom and guidance for the day according to Proverbs 3:5-6,

Trust in the Lord with all thine heart and lean not unto thine own understanding. In all thy ways acknowledge Him, and He shall direct thy paths.

We thank You, Father, that each student will witness within their spirit the importance of putting on the full armor of God each day (as instructed in Ephesians 6:10-18), so that they will be prepared for spiritual warfare. Your Word says in Ephesians 6:12 that ...*we wrestle not against flesh and blood, but against principalities, against powers, against the rulers of the darkness of this world, against spiritual wickedness in high places.* We thank You, Father, that as they put on the Helmet of Salvation, their minds are protected from the evil one; their minds are kept in perfect peace.

Your Word says in 1 Corinthians 2:16, *For who hath known the mind of the Lord, that he may instruct Him? But we have the mind of Christ.* And in Isaiah 26:3 we read, *Thou will keep him in perfect peace, whose mind is stayed on Thee: because he trusteth in Thee.* We declare that the students' minds will stay on You so that there will be no thoughts of depression, self-pity, or suicide.

We thank You, Father, that the students will come into the knowledge of You as their covenant Father, and that they are Your covenant children by the Blood shed at Calvary. Thank You, Father, that they realize they are made in Your image according to Genesis 1:26, and that You have plans for them to be successful. (Psalm 1:3)

We thank You, Father, that as they seek Your wisdom and spiritual discernment according to Proverbs 1:2-5, they will be able to listen to the voice of the Holy Spirit guiding them away from friendships that will only lead to corruption (1 Corinthians 15:33-34)—those that would keep them from receiving the spiritual growth You desire for them.

Father, we pray Your Word over these students regarding finances and employment. In Isaiah 48:17, Your Word says You are the Lord God who teaches them to profit and who leads them by the way they should go. We thank You, Father, that these students will find honest employment according to 2 Thessalonians 3:10, so that all their needs are met and that they may walk honestly toward those who are without. We also pray that they will bring their tithes into Your storehouse as Malachi 3:10 tells them to do.

Father, for single students who are praying for a helpmate, we pray that they will take time to study Your Word (as in Genesis 24:12-14, 2 Corinthians 6:14). I pray that Your Holy Spirit will make them sensitive to wait and allow You, Father, to lead in this important decision.

We thank You now for pouring out Your blessings, Your presence, and Your power on these students. It is in Jesus' Name we pray. AMEN.

PRAYER FOR HEALING

My Father God, in the Name of Jesus, over and over in Your Word, You have shown us that it is Your will for us to be healed—that we do not have to "wonder" if it is Your will. We stand on Your promises for healing as part of our inheritance. You said, *for I am the Lord that healeth thee.* Jesus was made sick with our diseases that we be made whole. We know that Jesus only said and did what pleased You and Jesus gave His disciples power over all manner of sickness. So we, too, walk in that authority and say "*by His stripes, we were healed.*" We speak to our minds and every part of our bodies and command them to line up with the Word of God.

We choose to stand on Your promises in Your Word commanding healing, rather than the dictates of our flesh. In Galatians 3:13, Your Word says, *Christ hath redeemed us from the curse of the law, being made a curse for us: for it is written, Cursed is every one that hangeth on a tree.* So, we declare that we have been delivered from the curse of the law which is sin, sickness, disease, and lack in our lives. We forbid any sickness or disease to operate in our bodies. We declare that every organ, every tissue of our bodies functions in the perfection in which God created it to function. We honor God and bring glory to Him in our bodies. *Jesus bore our sins in His own body on the tree, that we, being dead to sins, should live unto righteousness: by whose stripes ye were healed.* (1 Peter 2:24) Thank You, God, for the Blood of Jesus! We receive all that was provided for us at Calvary.

Father, we thank You, too, for Your promises in Psalm 91:1, 10-11 for peace and security: *He that dwelleth in the secret place of the Most High shall abide under the shadow of the Almighty... There shall no evil befall thee, neither shall any plague come nigh thy dwelling, For He shall give His angels charge over thee to keep thee in all thy ways.*

We thank You, Father, for Psalm 73:26 that says,...*but God is the strength of my heart, and my portion forever.* We stand on Your Word and command our hearts to line up with the Word of God, that our hearts must be strong and not weak!

We stir up the anointing for the fruit of the Spirit to be alive in us so that we walk in love and forgiveness with joy so that we give no place to the devil. Satan, it gives our Father great pleasure for us to rebuke you and we command you to leave and leave now and take all your symptoms of infirmity of any kind with you. We have authority over you—we submit ourselves to God—we resist you and you <u>have</u> to flee—now get!

Now, Father, in Jesus' Name, we give You all glory, honor, and praise for strong, healthy minds and bodies! AMEN.

Matthew 8:17—This verse reveals that He was made sick with our diseases that we may be made <u>whole</u>.

Exodus 15:26	1 Corinthians 2:16
John 8:28-29	Galatians 5:22-23
Matthew 10:1	James 4:7
1 Peter 2:24	Ephesians 4:27
3 John 2	Psalm 25:14

PRAYERS INDIVIDUALS MAY PRAY WHEN THEY HAVE BUSY SCHEDULES

FOR MARRIED INDIVIDUALS

NOTE: This is a five to ten minute prayer. It is written especially for a married person with children who is "on-the-go," who loves Jesus, who has not taken the time to develop a prayer time but desires to talk with God before starting the day.

Father God, I come to You in the Name of Jesus and by the Blood shed at Calvary, and I thank You that I have another day to serve You, to praise You, and to worship You. I love You, and I want to be a blessing to You today. The desire of my heart is for You to be top priority in my life—not my husband, wife, or my children, or job—for Your Word says in Deuteronomy 6:5 and Matthew 22:37, *Thou shalt love the Lord thy God with all thine heart, and with all thy soul, and with all thy mind.*

Father, I ask You now to forgive me when my love is not in line with Your Word. I want to yield to the leading of Your precious

Holy Spirit so that He may teach me how to praise and worship You and how to glorify Jesus—and that He may teach me how to keep the love in my heart pure toward You and, then, toward my helpmate and my children.

Holy Spirit, thank You for guiding me and directing me with God's wisdom in every decision that needs to be made today. I need Your spiritual discernment according to God's Word in Proverbs 1:1-5 and in James 1:5-8. I know that no person can satisfy the desires of my heart (Psalm 37:4-5), but when I put my complete confidence and trust in You (Proverbs 3:5-6), You fulfill the longings in my heart and keep the motives of my heart pure. *You are the strength of my heart and my portion forever.* (Psalm 73:26)

I pray a hedge of protection around myself and my family. Thank You, Father, for fulfilling the call on their lives. Thank You for my children, and I declare that my seed are the seed of the righteous. (Psalm 112:2) I confess that my children obey and honor their parents and because of this, they may live long on the earth. (Ephesians 6:1-3) As a parent, I do not want to provoke or irritate my children or to wound their spirit man. (Ephesians 6:4) I do not want to discourage them in any way but to help them see themselves as You see them. They are made in Your image (Genesis 1:26), Father, and I want them to be filled with Your love and Your joy so that they will be a blessing to You and to others.

Father, thank You for my pastor and his family. Thank You for sending this shepherd to guide and feed the sheep. Holy Spirit of God, I thank You for giving our pastor wisdom, guidance, comfort, and strength that he needs for this day. Father, I thank You for raising up mighty prayer warriors that will be faithful to pray for him and to stand in the gap for him every day.

Thank You, Father, for my church. I pray for a spirit of prayer, unity, love, giving, and revival to continue sweeping over my church. Bring people from the North, South, East, and West who will flow in one accord with the vision that You have for the Body of Christ. We want Your plans and purposes for the church, not ours!

Give me an opportunity today to be a blessing to You, Father, and the Body of Christ. Only You can give my life real meaning and purpose.

It is in Jesus' Name I pray. AMEN.

PRAYERS FOR PARENTS WITH REBELLIOUS TEENAGERS

Father, we come to You in the Name of Jesus. We come into Your courts with thanksgiving and into Your Gates with praise. We cannot hide anything from You; only You know that we do not "feel" like praising and worshipping, but we tell our "feelings" to be quiet! We declare that we are overcomers in this situation, and in every situation, by the Blood of Jesus that was shed at Calvary according to Your Word in Revelation 12:11, *And they overcame him by the Blood of the Lamb, and by the word of their testimony: and they loved not their lives unto the death.*

You, Father, are our total source of supply: You are our comforter, our shield, our protection, and our security. By faith, Father, we ask for Your wisdom, and we know that it will be given to us because of Your Word in James 1:5, *If any of you lack wisdom, let him ask of God, that giveth to all men liberally, and upbraideth not and it shall be given him.*

We, as parents, have taken our responsibility seriously. We feel we have done all that we could do to raise our children in a godly manner. In whatever areas we have failed, we ask Your forgiveness and ask that You point out those areas in our lives that are in need of change so that we can be quick to repent, *For if we would judge ourselves, we should not be judged.* (1 Corinthians 11:31)

We refuse to let strife and hostility settle in our home. Strife and hostility are demonic forces, and we bind them now in Jesus' Name and declare that they will not operate in our home. *Let us walk honestly, as in the day: not in rioting and drunkenness, not in chambering and wantonness, not in strife and envying.* (Romans 13:13)

Father, Your Word says in 1 Corinthians 13:7 (Amplified), *Love bears up under anything and everything that comes, is ever ready to believe the best of every person, its hopes are fadeless under all circumstances, and it endures everything (without weakening).* So, we purpose in our hearts to walk in love toward this child that we do not understand at this time.

In Psalm 112:2, You say that *my seed shall be mighty upon the earth,* and in verse 7, *He shall not be afraid of evil tidings, his heart is fixed, trusting in the Lord.* We stand on these promises in Your Word. In Isaiah 55:11, it says, *Your word will not return unto You void but will accomplish that which You please.*

In Philippians 4:6-7, Your Word says, *Be careful for nothing: but in everything by prayer and supplication with thanksgiving let your requests be made known unto God. And the peace of God which passeth all understanding, shall keep your hearts and minds through Christ Jesus.* Your Word, Father, is a comfort to us every day, and we have purposed in our hearts to stand on Your promises, knowing full well that You will never leave us nor forsake us.

In Psalm 138:8 You say, *The Lord will perfect that which concerneth me.* We know that You will perfect that which concerns us, and we put the care of our children into Your hands. We refuse to be anxious about this situation any more. We choose to give You all glory, honor, and praise for all that You are in our lives, and we declare that Jesus is Lord of our home!

In Jesus' Name we pray. AMEN.

PRAYER FOR CHILDREN OF A BROKEN HOME

Father God, we come to You in the name of Your Son, Jesus, and by the Blood shed at Calvary. We want to pray for

_____ , _____ and _____

We desire that this prayer be for every boy and girl whose life has been affected by strife in the home where they have been raised. Father, we know there are wounds that need healing. Jesus, You are the only One who can minister to them. 1 Peter 2:24 says, *Who His own self bare our sins in His own body on the tree, that we, being dead to sins, should live unto righteousness:*

137

by whose stripes ye were healed. Thank You for being Jehovah-Rapha, the Lord that heals!

Father, Your Son, Jesus, knew what it was like to feel lonely, and to feel rejected. Everything that we have experienced has already been experienced by Jesus—He has already been there. Now He wants to be our friend and bring love and comfort into our lives. He wants us to rise above the circumstances of life and be filled with His joy, *And now come I to Thee: and these things I speak in the world, that they might have My joy fulfilled in themselves.* (John 17:13) In Nehemiah 8:10 You say, *the joy of the Lord is our strength.*

We thank You, Father, for Your Word says that our total source of security is in Jesus Christ. Truly Jesus is greater in us than the devil that is causing the hurt in the families, *My sheep hear My voice, and I know them, and they follow Me. And I give unto them eternal life; and they shall never perish, neither shall any man pluck them out of My hand. My Father which gave them Me, is greater than all; and no man is able to pluck them out of My Father's hand.* (John 10:27-29) You, Father, are greater than any problem any of Your children will ever have. Let them put their trust in You this day.

Thank You, Father, for letting them know the comfort they seek is found in Your Word and in Your presence. (Psalm 91) Let them see, as in Psalm 23, that You are their Shepherd, the One who leads and guides them, the One who heals and restores, Jehovah-Rapha. Holy Spirit of God, we thank You now for sweeping across their hearts and healing them spiritually, physically, and mentally.

We thank You, Father, The boys and girls for whom we pray will get a new image of themselves and begin to see themselves as You created them to be, *And God said, Let Us make man in Our image after Our likeness.* (Genesis 1:26) We thank You that they are created in Your image and that You have a special plan and purpose for their life. As they keep their eyes on Jesus, they will learn to live above the hurts that have struck so deeply and will know that they can be delivered from those hurts.

We pray that these children will daily yield to the Holy Spirit and receive the comfort, strength, help, and security that His fellowship can bring. Father, we pray that as they grow closer and closer to You, they will begin to walk in love, the kind of love You speak of in 1 Corinthians 13. Thank You that there is a desire in their heart to develop that type of unselfish love and to walk in forgiveness toward those who have caused so much hurt in their lives. By Your grace they have been forgiven, and now they need to see the need to forgive others.

Father, we thank You for sending laborers across the path of the parents, to witness to them how much Jesus loves them so that they, too, may feel Your forgiveness and the security of Your love. Please let them know that once they have received Jesus as their Lord, they are not to receive a spirit of condemnation, for Your Word says, *There is therefore now no condemnation to them which are in Christ Jesus, who walk not after the flesh, but after the Spirit. For the law of the Spirit of life in Christ Jesus hath made me free from the law of sin and death.* (Romans 8:1-2)

Thank You now, Father, for You and for Your Son, Jesus, and for the precious Holy Spirit. Thank You for drawing these children (regardless of their age, for we are all Your covenant children) under Your wing and into that secret place where they may abide. (Psalm 91) Let them know and stand on the promises that are in Your Word and feel the presence of Your Holy Spirit in their lives each day.

We thank You in advance for comforting these precious children. It is in Jesus' Name we pray. AMEN.

PRAYER FOR HEALING OF A MARRIAGE

Father, we come to You in the Name of Your Son, Jesus, and we lift up to You the marriage of _____ and _____. Father, we see in Isaiah 54:17 that it says, *No weapon that is formed against thee shall prosper and every tongue that shall rise against thee in judgment Thou shalt condemn. This is the heritage of the servants of the Lord, and their righteousness is of Me, saith the Lord.* Father, we claim this scripture now for this couple, and we apply Your promises to their marriage. Right now we come against any negative words that may have been spoken about this marriage, and we declare these words to be null and void. Also, we claim Your promise in Colossians 1:20, *And, having made peace through the Blood of His cross, by Him to reconcile all things unto Himself: by Him, I say, whether they be things in earth, or things in heaven.*

Right now, Father, we speak reconciliation to this marriage because the power of reconciliation is one of the precious benefits God's covenant children receive through the Blood of Jesus shed at Calvary.

We pray that Jehovah-Shalom will minister the unity of the Lord Jesus in that home so that they may experience love, peace, and forgiveness in their marriage. We claim 1 Corinthians 1:10, *Now I beseech you, brethren, by the Name of our Lord Jesus Christ, that ye all speak the same thing, and that there be no divisions among you; but that ye be perfectly joined together in the same mind and in the same judgment.*

Thank You, Father, that they will forgive one another as Christ forgave them—that they will be tenderhearted toward one another—that their marriage will be stronger than ever with Jesus as the Lord of their home.

Satan, we speak to you in the Name of Jesus, and we command you to call off your demons that have been assigned to this marriage. Those demons of strife and division that cause thoughts of separation and divorce, we tell you that your assignment is over because of the authority we have in Christ Jesus over you. We command you to leave this couple NOW and to never return in the Name of Jesus!

Thank You, Father, for restoring this marriage. Thank You that Your love ("Hesed" and "Agape") never fails. We declare that Jesus is Lord of this marriage! It is in Jesus' Name that we pray. AMEN.

PRAYER THOUGHTS

We would have less break-ups of homes and less problems in the homes if husbands would assume their position as the spiritual authority in the home. What a Godly heritage and security Fathers would give their children to be seen reading the Bible and spending time on their knees praying.

"The man who mobilizes the Christian Church to pray will make the greatest contribution to the world evangelism in history."

- Andrew Murray -

"I would rather teach one man to pray than to teach ten men to preach."

- Charles H. Spurgeon -

"The one concern of the devil is to keep Christians from praying. He fears nothing from prayerless studies, prayerless work, and prayerless religion. He laughs at our toil, mocks at our wisdom, but trembles when we pray!"

- Sam Chadwick -

"If I could hear Christ praying for me in the next room, I would not fear a million enemies. Yet, the distance makes no difference. He is praying for me!"

- Robert Murray McCheyne -

"We need to talk less and pray more."

"The best prayer warriors are found in the prayer closets!"

"There are no 'instant' prayer warriors!"

"You cannot really 'reach out' until you 'reach up!'"

"No church can be called a praying church until it meets more to pray for others than it does to pray for itself."

"No church can be called a missionary church until it spends more upon others than it does upon itself."

"If prayer is God's top priority, then prayer must become the church's top priority!"

"Prayerless marriages do not make a home."

"Children without praying fathers are spiritual orphans."

"Prayer changes your countenance!"

"If you love your wife, husband, children, girlfriend or boyfriend, Mother or Father more than you love Jesus, you will always have trouble with your prayer life!"

"Wives without praying husbands are spiritual widows."

"A true prayer warrior spends more time with his Commander-in-Chief and less time in the battle!"

NOTES

LESSON 17
PEOPLE WHO YIELDED
TO A LIFE OF PRAYER

INTRODUCTION

In this chapter, I have listed only a few of the many people who yielded to a life of prayer. There are many, many more, and I would encourage you to make a study of great prayer warriors. They all have something with which to build you up and encourage you in your walk with the Lord.

Before we begin studying some of the great men and women who dared to trust God, we need to keep in mind that these people were real human beings like you and like me! We, too, can dare to trust God, to believe that the promises in His Word were written for us to live by, backed by the power of the Blood shed at Calvary. You can step out every day, leaning on, and trusting in the guidance of the Holy Spirit within you, causing you to be victorious in every situation.

Our God is the God of the impossible! Put your faith and trust in Him and not in man! Nothing, absolutely nothing, is impossible with God.

I.   JESUS

Let's begin this chapter with Jesus. We owe our prayer lives to the pattern He lived for us.

A. Prayer was top priority in Jesus' life. He lived His life in communion with His Father. Jesus Christ, the Son of God, believed in prayer and we need to follow His example:

1. Jesus Prayed Before Daybreak.

Mark 1:35, *And in the morning, rising up a great while before day, He went out, and departed into a solitary place, and there prayed.*

2. Jesus Spent All Night In Prayer.

Luke 6:12, *And it came to pass in those days, that He went out into a mountain to pray, and continued all night in prayer to God.*

3. Jesus Prayed Privately.

Matthew 14:23, *And when He had sent the multitudes away He went up into a mountain apart to pray: and when the evening was come, He was there alone.*

4. Jesus Was The Master of Prayer.

His disciples went with Him from one prayer meeting to another, and they saw the power of God flowing out from Him to meet every need. Luke 11:1 tells us that Jesus was praying one day, and when He stopped praying, they said, *Lord, teach us to pray, as John also taught his disciples.*

    a. In Matthew 6:9-13, Jesus taught His disciples to pray what we refer to as the Lord's Prayer:

    v. 9, *After this manner therefore pray ye: Our Father which art in heaven. Hallowed be Thy name.*

    v. 10, *Thy kingdom come. Thy will be done in earth, as it is in heaven.*

    v. 11, *Give us this day our daily bread.*

    v. 12, *And forgive us our debts, as we forgive our debtors.*

    v. 13, *And lead us not into temptation, but deliver us from evil: For Thine is the kingdom, and the power, and the glory, forever. Amen.*

5. Jesus Prayed Over Jerusalem.

Matthew 23:37, *O, Jerusalem, Jerusalem, thou that killest the prophets, and stonest them which are sent unto thee, how often would I have gathered thy children together, even as a hen gathereth her chickens under her wings, and ye would not!*

B. Jesus' High-Priestly Prayer.

One of the most beautiful prayers ever prayed in the history of the world is found in John 17. Jesus made love and unity His top priority. If we receive the love He prayed for us to have toward one another, then the unity in the Lord Jesus will follow!

1. We see in the following verses that Jesus had accomplished on earth all that He was sent to do, with the exception of planting the seed of His life on Calvary (since He was the seed of David). He is praying that His followers would come into the unity of the body and experience the love and joy that He walked in while He was with them. (John 17:1-4)

   v. 1, *These words spake Jesus, and lifted up His eyes to heaven, and said, Father, the hour is come; glorify Thy Son, that Thy Son also may glorify Thee.*

   v. 2, As *Thou hast given Him power over all flesh, that He should give eternal life to as many as Thou hast given Him.*

   v. 3, *And this is life eternal, that they might know Thee the only true God, and Jesus Christ, whom Thou hast sent.*

   v. 4, *I have glorified Thee on the earth: I have finished the work which Thou gavest Me to do.*

2. There is tremendous power in unity! Not just any unity, but the unity of the Lord Jesus Christ. In the days we are living in, the Body of Christ must learn to flow in the unity that Jesus prayed to His Father we would have. In the following verses Jesus prays specifically that we might be one as He and His Father are one. (John 17:5-11)

145

v. 5, *And now, 0 Father glorify Thou Me with Thine own self with the glory which I had with Thee before the world was.*

v. 6, *I have manifested Thy name unto the men which Thou gavest me out of the world: Thine they were, and Thou gavest them Me; and they have kept Thy word.*

v. 7, *Now they have known that all things whatsoever Thou hast given Me are of Thee.*

v. 8, *For I have given unto them the words which Thou gavest me; and they have received them, and have known surely that I came out from Thee, and they have believed that Thou didst send Me.*

v. 9, *I pray for them: I pray not for the world, but for them which Thou hast given Me; for they are Thine.*

v. 10, *And all Mine are Thine, and Thine are Mine, and I am glorified in them.*

v. 11, *And now I am no more in the world, but these are in the world, and I come to Thee. Holy Father keep through Thine own Name those whom Thou hast given Me, that they may be one, as We are.*

3. The Bible tells us the joy of the Lord is our strength. The heavenly joy that Jesus' Father had given Him would give Him the strength to face the cross. Jesus realized His disciples would be living in a hostile world where they would need to be filled with heavenly joy in order to face the different trials that would come their way. (John 17:12-13) Joy is a fruit of the Spirit and is mentioned in all four gospels. Joy manifested in a Christian's life— no matter the situation or circumstance—is a sign of spiritual maturity.

v. 12, *While I was with them in the world, I kept them in Thy name: those that Thou gavest Me I have kept, and none of them is lost, but the son of perdition; that the scripture might be fulfilled.*

v. 13, *And now come I to Thee; and these things I speak in the world, that they might have My joy fulfilled in themselves.*

4. Jesus was praying for us that we may have a unity together in Christ so that we might spiritually affect those unbelievers in the world. He has given us the power to affect unbelievers. In the following verses, especially verses 20 and 21, we see that Jesus included you and me and future believers in His prayer. (John 17:14-21)

v. 14, *I have given them Thy word; and the world hath hated them, because they are not of the world, even as I am not of the world.*

v. 15, *I pray not that Thou shouldest take them out of the world, but that Thou shouldest keep them from the evil.*

v. 16, *They are not of the world, even as I am not of the world.*

v. 17, *Sanctify them through Thy truth: Thy word is truth.*

NOTE: Here we see Jesus praying, that His disciples would be set apart for service to God.

v. 18, *As Thou hast sent Me into the world, even so have I also sent them into the world.*

v. 19, *And for their sakes, I sanctify Myself that they also might be sanctified through the truth.*

v. 20, *Neither pray I for these alone but for them also which shall believe on Me through their word.*

v. 21, *That they all may be one; as Thou, Father, art in Me, and I in Thee, that they also may be one in Us: that the world may believe that Thou hast sent Me.*

5. In the following verses, Jesus speaks of "Agape" love—the kind of love that we show one another in spite of our differences. We cannot do this by ourselves, or in the natural, but we can do it through Jesus loving through us. We must have unity and brotherly love. (John 17:22-23)

v. 22, *And the glory which Thou gavest Me I have given them; that they may be one, even as We are one.*

v. 23, *I in them, and Thou in Me, that they may be made perfect in one; and that the world may know that Thou hast sent Me, and hast loved them, as Thou hast loved Me.*

6. In the following verses we see Jesus praying for us.

After this beautiful intercessory prayer, Jesus had supernatural strength, poise, and control to handle the situation that was to follow as Judas betrays Him and brings a band of accusers to the Garden of Gethsemane. (John 17:24-26)

v. 24, *Father, I will that they also, whom Thou hast given Me, be with Me where I am; that they may behold My glory, which Thou hast given Me: for Thou lovedst Me before the foundation of the world.*

v. 25, *O righteous Father, the world hath not known Thee: but I have known Thee and these have known that Thou hast sent Me.*

v 26, *And I have declared unto them Thy Name, and will declare it that the love wherewith Thou hast loved Me may be in them, and I in them.*

II. ABRAHAM

Abraham was a friend to God. He is called the pioneer of faith. We, too, can have the faith of Abraham.

A. As we spend time with God, our faith grows stronger. In Genesis 12:1-3 we read:

v. 1, *Now the Lord had said unto Abram, Get thee out of thy country, and from thy kindred, and from thy father's house, unto a land that I will shew thee.*

v. 2, *And I will make of thee a great nation, and I will bless thee, and make thy name great and thou shalt be a blessing.*

v. 3, *And I will bless them that bless thee, and curse him that curseth thee: and in thee shall all families of the earth be blessed.*

B. We see God's promises are clear, and at age 75, Abram moves his family to an unknown place. As he obediently leaves his home, God repeats the promises. (Genesis 13:14-16) Abram followed God BEFORE the promises ever seemed attainable. You and I, as well, can walk in that kind of faith and have the understanding of the fullness of God's plans and purposes for our lives opened up before us. We need to come to the place in our faith walk that age is of no concern—we must believe in God's promises and be quick to do what He tells us to do—have the faith of a little child. (Matthew 18:3-4, Luke 18:16-17)

   1. Godly faith is an investment of your life, and that investment yields great dividends. Abraham and Sarah invested their lives in following God, and their returns have continued to multiply even to this day. (Galatians 3:8-9, Hebrews 11:6)

C. When Abraham arrived in Canaan, he pitched a tent and built an altar. At this time, God renewed His promise, and Abram was assured that he was on the right road. After the battle of the kings, Abraham, returned to Mamre. (Genesis 15-17) God spoke to him and said, *Fear not Abram: I am thy shield, and thy exceeding great reward.* (Genesis 15:1) Abraham steadied himself by leaning on God: and in return, God imputed character to him.

D. God's closeness with Abraham is duplicated many times over in people who understand their spiritual roots and stand confidently before the Lord in prayer. (Ephesians 1:4-7; 3:20) As you grow in your understanding of prayer, being timid before God will turn to humble confidence!

E. In Genesis 18:23-32, we read about Abraham's great intercession for the cities of Sodom and Gomorrah.

F. Things we can learn from Abraham's life:

1. **Talk to God**. Abraham felt comfortable enough in God's presence to plead for a sinful city. God cares about your concerns. (Psalm 138:8, Philippians 4:6-7)

2. **Walk with God**. Abraham's walk with God taught him God's plan. Learn to move in the direction God is going. (Colossians 1:9-10)

3. **Watch for God**. Listen to Him as you read the scriptures and as you sing spiritual songs. (Romans 1:20)

4. **Wait on God**. God's plans are bigger and better than ours. (Isaiah 55:8-9) Abraham's concern for Lot moved God to mercy. Those who wait on God, experience His peace. (Isaiah 26:3) Pray that we will follow God's plans and not man's plans.

III. MOSES

In Deuteronomy 34:10 we read, *And there arose not a prophet since in Israel like unto Moses, whom the Lord knew face to face.*

A. The call of Moses (Exodus 3-4), Moses was on the backside of the desert tending to his father-in-law's sheep when God appeared to him. For forty years in Egypt, Moses had learned the skills of the educated person. Compared to all the privileges he enjoyed in the royal court, life in the desert must have been lonely.

Yet, there in the desert for forty years, he was taught the qualities of spiritual leadership: patience, maturity, and sensitivity to the voice of God.

1. God spoke to Moses from a bush that was on fire, but it did not burn. (Exodus 3:2) God revealed Himself to Moses as the God of Abraham, Isaac, and Jacob at Horeb. God revealed Himself to Moses as Yahweh, I AM THAT I AM. (Exodus 3:14-15)

2. God told Moses that He would deliver the Israelites from their suffering. He called Moses to go and lead them out of Egypt, to lead them out of bondage because of His covenant with Abraham. God promised Moses He would be with him. (Exodus 3:7-12) God told Moses to tell the Israelites that Yahweh, the God of Abraham, Isaac, and Jacob, had promised to bring them out of Egypt and into the land of Canaan. (Exodus 3:13-17)

3. The Amalekites attacked the Israelites at Rephidim. The Israelites defeated them while Moses prayed (Exodus 17:8-13), and God's presence brought victory. Moses built an altar and named it *The Lord my banner* (Jehovah-Nissi). What Moses was really saying was "We did not win the victory only because Joshua fought and I prayed, but we won because God was with us and He helped us."

B. Things We Can Learn From Moses' Life:

1. God will make Himself known to people. Moses was tending sheep—he was not expecting anything unusual to happen. He was not seeking God, but God was seeking Moses. God spoke to Moses, and Moses' whole life was changed.

2. As Moses was obedient to do what God asked of him, he came to know God more fully.

3. God calls people, gives them a task to do and then gives them the power and equipment to accomplish

that task. When God wanted to set the Israelites free from Egypt, He chose Moses. But Moses did not want to go to the Pharaoh of Egypt—he did not feel capable of that task. (Exodus 3:11) God, however, had promised to be with him. (Exodus 3:12)

4. Moses was one of the great intercessors in the Bible.

NOTE: When we have God's presence and God's power, we are able to serve Him and do what He wants us to do, and we know we have God's presence with us at all times in the form of the Holy Spirit—the eternal life of God living on the inside of us!

IV. JOSHUA

Joshua is named for the first time in Exodus 17:9, *And Moses said unto Joshua, choose us out men, and go out, fight with Amalek.*

A. The Israelites had crossed the Red Sea in their flight from Egypt, and a few days later had come to Rephidim. (Exodus 17) There the people began to murmur against God. Moses, by God's direction, smote the rock and God provided water. Almost immediately after this, the Amalekites came against the Israelites to make war with them. It was then that Joshua was made a general of the forces of the Lord—a role that would immediately begin to teach Joshua that God would not tolerate the rebellion of men against Himself: *Because the hand of Amalek is against the throne of the Lord therefore hath the Lord sworn, the Lord will have war with Amalek from generation to generation.* Joshua quickly found that real power is in the power of God, and not in the power of his role as general, or in the sword he carried.

NOTE: After reading these scriptures, notice the faith and obedience of Joshua. Moses called for Joshua and commanded him to organize the armies and attack the Amalekites. Without questions or objections, he organized the untrained soldiers of Israel and fought the Amalekites. It was not the fighting skill of the Israelites that brought victory, but it was the consistent prayers of Moses.

B. Joshua was on Mount Sinai, while Moses was at the top of the mountain as God wrote the Ten Commandments (in His own handwriting) on the tablets of stone.

C. Also in Exodus 33:9, 11, we read the following account:

v. 9, *And it came to pass, as Moses entered into the tabernacle, and the Lord talked with Moses.*

v. 11, *And the Lord spake unto Moses face to face, as a man speaketh unto his friend. And he turned again into the camp: but his servant Joshua, the son of Nun, a young man, departed not out of the tabernacle.*

   1. Moses was truly a different type of person; Joshua was being trained, in this unusual situation, by a man who had been face-to-face with God. Joshua was being prepared for future leadership as he learned the reality of God in His glory—that God not only could but would guide him in every situation as he prayed and stayed in close fellowship with Him.

D. *And if it seem evil unto you to serve the Lord, choose you this day whom ye will serve: whether the gods which your fathers served that were on the other side of the flood, or the gods of the Amorites, in whose land ye dwell: but as for me and my house, we will serve the Lord.* (Joshua 24:15)

   1. Joshua made this choice every day as he was yielding to preparation for serving God. God taught Joshua many things as Joshua followed Moses in the wilderness. Usually, there is preparation before leadership, and true spiritual leadership does not come from the hands of men, but from God.

V. DAVID

David means "Beloved." He began his life as a shepherd boy, tending to his father's sheep. It was during that time that David's close walk with God became a part of him.

A. David knew his God would keep him from all harm.

   1. He knew first-hand how his God had delivered him out of the paw of the lion and out of the paw of the bear while he was on the hillside tending sheep. (1 Samuel 17:37)

   2. He knew that his God would cause him to again be victorious as he went out against Goliath, the uncircumcised Philistine, who was defying the armies of the living God. (1 Samuel 17:26) His victory over Goliath was the turning point of his career.

B. David was one of the greatest prayer warriors in history.

   In Psalm 40:1 we read, *I waited patiently for the Lord: and He inclined unto me, and heard my cry.*

   In Psalm 63:1-2 he wrote, *O God, Thou art my God; early will I seek Thee: my soul thirsteth for Thee, my flesh longeth for Thee in a dry and thirsty land, where no water is.*

   v. 2, *To see Thy power and Thy glory, so as I have seen Thee in the sanctuary.*

C. David is described as a man after God's own heart. His mind was stayed on God. He knew the secret of seeking the Lord and the refreshing he would experience as he sat in His presence.

   1. My soul shall be satisfied as with marrow and fatness; and my mouth shall praise Thee with joyful lips. (Psalm 63:5) The top priority in David's life was to stay close to God, My soul followeth hard after Thee: Thy right hand upholdeth me. (Psalm 63:8)

VI. ANNA

Anna prayed daily, *And she was a widow of about fourscore and four years, which departed not from the temple, but served God with fastings and prayers night and day.* (Luke 2:36-38)

VII. HANNAH

Hannah was childless. She prayed earnestly to God and He answered her prayer with the birth of Samuel. And she vowed a vow, and said, *O Lord of hosts, if Thou wilt indeed look on the affliction of Thine handmaid, and remember me, and not forget Thine handmaid, but wilt give unto Thine handmaid a man child, then I will give him unto the Lord all the days of his life and there shall no razor come upon his head.* (1 Samuel 1:11)

VIII. JOHN WESLEY

John Wesley, the founder of Methodistism, was born in Epworth, England, in 1703 and died in 1791. He has been dead now for over 200 years, but because he dared to believe the promises of God (he dared to believe in prayer, walking by faith, and miraculous healings), it has been said that the life and teachings of John Wesley have had as great an influence on the Church as any since the days of the apostle Paul.

A. John Wesley inspired the Methodist movement, and it spread worldwide until it became the largest body in Protestantism. No minister living in the Eighteenth Century traveled as much as he did. "The world is my parish," was his famous motto. He carried the good news on horseback throughout England, Scotland, and Ireland. He often traveled on horseback, carriage, and sailing vessels as much as 8,000 miles a year. Sometimes he walked as far as twenty-five miles a day to his preaching engagements. He did much of his reading while walking or on horseback.

B. For sixty years he arose at four o'clock every morning and spent hours in prayer before God. He was always refreshed for his days' work.

C. John Wesley believed in the power of the supernatural. His understanding of these things began during a storm at sea, when he witnessed the remarkable spiritual calm of the Moravians, even though it seemed disaster was about to strike. They believed God could and would intervene for their protection from the fury of the sea, and he realized they possessed a faith he did not. From that time on he began to seek God for a deeper experience in his own life.

D. Not long after his experience with the Moravians, John Wesley received a definite heart-felt conversion to Christ. Later he received a mighty anointing of the Spirit during an all-night prayer meeting. He writes: "About three o'clock (a.m.) we were in prayer, the power of God came mightily upon us, insomuch that many cried out in exceeding joy, and many fell to the ground." This event marked the beginning of the Great Awakening in England.

E. John Wesley believed in God's promises for healing. In his journal he records over two hundred cases of miraculous healings. He understood the cause of sickness and knew that in many cases an illness could be caused by demon oppression or possession. Of one poor woman attacked with fits he said, "The plain case is, she is tormented by an evil spirit; yea, try all your drugs over and over, but at length it will plainly appear, 'This kind goeth not out but by prayer and fasting.'" Miraculous deliverances occurred in his ministry.

F. On one occasion, he was preaching outside and the sun was exceedingly hot. He prayed that God would help him so that he would not have to dismiss the service. In a few minutes the sky was covered with clouds, and it stayed that way until the service ended. He said, "Let anyone who please call this chance; I call it an answer to prayer."

G. John Wesley made fasting a part of his own personal discipline. He encouraged the Methodists to fast every Wednesday and Friday. In fact, he would not ordain to the Methodist ministry any man who would not undertake to fast until 4:00 p.m. each Wednesday and Friday.

H. The Methodist movement owes its origin to John Wesley, a man who firmly believed in a ministry of the supernatural. What a shame that many of his followers were willing to benefit from the work of this man and serve pulpits in his movement, but they did not share the faith of its founder and were embarrassed by Wesley's belief in these things.

   1. One of John Wesley's last statements before His death was: "There is no way into the holiest but by the Blood of Jesus."

   NOTE: Most Americans have forgotten their spiritual heritage just like the children of Israel forgot their heritage. God sent prophets to forestall judgment on Israel; in the nineteenth century God sent two great evangelists, Charles Finney and Dwight L. Moody, to bring America back on spiritual course.

IX. CHARLES G. FINNEY

In 1830, an attorney by the name of Charles G. Finney preached for six months at Rochester, New York, and saw 100,000 souls get saved.

A. Charles Finney was not raised in a godly home. As he was studying law, he noticed that his books contained many references to the Bible. He bought a Bible for reference but would always hide it with his other books when people were around! He visited a Presbyterian church and the congregation was praying for revival. He scorned and ridiculed all that was going on, but the young people in the church (led by the girl he would eventually marry) began praying for him. The Holy Spirit began to move on him and convict him of his sin. He could not eat or sleep. Finally, one afternoon he ran to the woods on the edge of town and poured out his sins before God. He ran back into town and shouted out the news of his salvation. Within twenty-four hours he had won twenty-four people to the Lord—among them another lawyer and a distiller!

B. Charles Finney dropped law and began to plead the cause of Jesus Christ. He began as an evangelist and took with him a man named Nash, who made prayer his all-consuming role. When Finney preached, Nash stayed behind and prayed. Every time he preached in London, in New York, or wherever, thousands accepted Jesus Christ as their Savior. In Boston, fifty thousand accepted Jesus in just one week!

X.   DWIGHT L. MOODY

In 1855, a dry-goods salesman in Boston led world famous Dwight L. Moody to the Lord in the back of a shoe store. Moody then moved west to Chicago and became a first rate shoe salesman!

A. Moody began traveling to the poor section of Chicago's north side, and before long his mission Sunday School took care of hundreds each week.

B. In 1873, Moody and his song leader, Ira Sankey, launched a campaign in the British Isles. Things started off slowly at first, but then they picked up, and thousands started being saved. The revival went to Edinburgh, Glasgow, and finally to London. The revival had such an impact that it was felt throughout England for years. When the campaign closed two years later, all of Great Britain was talking about Moody and Sankey.

PRAYER THOUGHT

America is hurting because of prayerlessness!

NOTES

To contact Ronnie Burch or
to order Prayer Manuals, write:

Barron (Ronnie) Burch
P.O. Box 5528
Cleveland, Tennessee 37320

Please include your prayer requests when you write.

Retailers and wholesalers should contact the publisher
(contact info on copyright page).